W9-CMR-681

10761
&BCM 1770

INTELLIGIBILITY AND THE PHILOSOPHY OF NOTHINGNESS

KITARŌ NISHIDA

Intelligibility and the Philosophy of Nothingness

Three Philosophical Essays

Translated with an Introduction by
Robert Schinzinger

East-West Center Press *Honolulu*

FERNALD LIBRARY
COLBY-SAWYER COLLEGE
NEW LONDON, N.H. 0325

B
5244
.N55
A313
1966

4/62

85320

© 1958 in Japan by the International Philosophical Research
Association of Japan

First published in 1958 by Maruzen Co., Ltd.
Second printing 1966

Printed and bound in Japan

Distributed outside Japan by
East-West Center Press, Honolulu

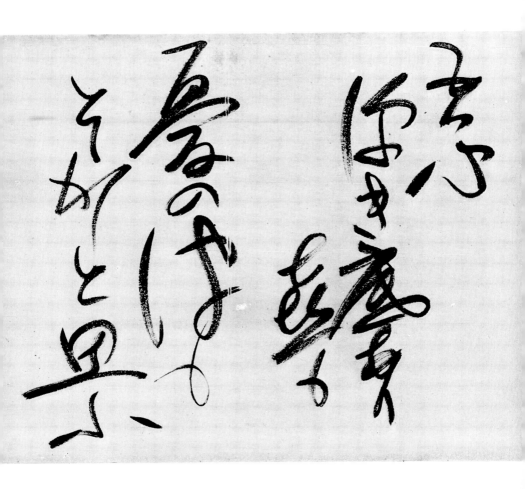

The bottom of my soul has such depth;
Neither joy nor the waves of sorrow can reach it.

PREFACE

While the history of Japanese metaphysical speculation, based on peculiarly Asian religious experiences, goes to the eleventh century, Japanese philosophy as organized in accordance with Western concepts and assumptions is barely a century old. Ever since they came in contact with the culture and philosophy of the West, Japanese thinkers have considered it their task to search for a harmonious integration of two philosophical worlds; to reformulate, in the categories of an alien Western philosophy, the philosophical insights of their own past. To have outlined one phase within this historical design is the achievement of Kitaro Nishida (1870–1945).

Nishida has written extensively on philosophy and his complete works fill twelve volumes. The present work consists of translations of three of his studies that all belong to a comparatively late phase in his development. Nishida has said of himself: "I have always been a miner of ore; I have never managed to refine it." The absence of a last systematic refinement may indeed be felt by the reader of the present selection. Still, the reader may be impressed by the strangely new experience of life here encountered, whether his heart is moved or his mind is made to think. Nishida uses Western concepts to express his philosophical reflection. The reader may not always perceive this, however, since Nishida's basic experience, with Zen at its center, cannot properly be formulated in Western terms and needs the structure of a new philosophical theory. The approach to his thought is, therefore, not easy. Yet we are convinced that Nishida's philosophy can open a new way towards the mutual understanding of East and West. In the hope of contributing to this mutual comprehension, upon which a new philosophy of mankind can be erected, we venture to offer the present publication to Western readers.

July, 1958

The International Philosophical Research
Association of Japan

3, Den-en-chofu 1, Ohta-ku, Tokyo

CONTENTS

INTRODUCTION

by

ROBERT SCHINZINGER

CHAPTER 1

The Difficulties of Understanding

This may not be the first time that the voice of Japan has been heard in the philosophical discussions of the West; but we still lack translations of modern Japanese philosophy. In attempting such a task, one must not overlook the fundamental difficulties of understanding the thoughts of a people so completely different in cultural and intellectual background. A philosophy cannot be separated from its historical setting. Like any other statement, a philosophical statement is related to the speaker, the listener, and the matter under discussion. It cannot, therefore, be completely isolated and separated from the background of both the speaker and the listener, nor from the continuity of the development of philosophical problems. And yet philosophical thought is not completely bound by that historical background, but reaches beyond it into a sphere of objectivity. In this realm of objectivity, we find the cold necessity of truth which simply does not allow of arbitrary statements. Any statement is somehow related to being. On the one hand, being is implied or involved in the subjective situation of speaker and listener; on the other hand, being is implied or involved in the discussed matter and its objectivity. Even if the standpoint of the speaker is very much different from that of the listener, the relationship to being should supply a common basis of discussion, and the relationship to being in the discussed matter should supply enough objectivity to compensate for the discrepancy in the national way of expression. After all, philosophy does not mean empty talk; philosophy is our intellectual struggle with problems whose particular structure does not depend solely on ourselves. Problems may have different meanings for different people, they may concern one more than another, but rarely are they completely imperceptible or inconceivable to others.

Even in listening to a voice which speaks to us from the depth of a different culture and existence, we cannot exclude the possibility of understanding the meta-logical elements of that alien culture.

It may seem unfamiliar to hear an oriental voice partaking in our familiar western discussion, but we must not eliminate the possibility of such participation. And we must not make the mistake of wanting to hear such a voice merely as an echo of our own voice (i.e. as eclecticism). And we must not make the other mistake of wanting to hear it as a thoroughly strange and therefore incomprehensible sound. It is true, however, that it requires a sensitive ear to hear that strange voice, for there is primarily a great difference in the way of delivering a speach. A good western speaker speaks loudly and clearly. A well educated Japanese speaks in a low voice. A western philosophical treatise must be outspoken, clear, and distinct, the analysis goes into every detail, and nothing should remain obscure. The Japanese loves the unspoken, he is content with giving subtle hints, just as in a Japanese black and white picture the white is sometimes more eloquent than the black. In the West it is different, for in a book all that is essential, is written there. Of course Westerners, too, can read between the lines, but for the Japanese it is very often the essential thing which is not said or written, and he hesitates to say what can be imagined or should be imagined. To a certain degree, he permits the reader to think for himself. The Westerner, on the other hand, wants to think for the reader. (This explains Schopenhauer's aversion to reading).

Another factor which makes Japanese writing and thinking so different from that of the West, is the use of Chinese characters, supplemented by two Japanese syllabic alphabets. The Japanese, in thinking, envisages these symbols which contain a tradition of several thousands of years. Their sight brings to the mind innumerable relations and nuances which may not be explicitly contained in the thought, but which form an emotional background. In the single symbolic character, something of the old magic of words is still alive. A translation can never reach the full significance which is represented to the Japanese mind by the sight of the Chinese character.

In all European languages, the meaning of a word

3

is clearly defined only through its function in the phrase, and by the context. In the Japanese language, however, the word preserves its independent meaning with little regard to context and functional position. Japanese grammar is comparatively loose and without much logical structure and adhesive power. The single character dominates in its visual form and its original meaning, enriched by Confucian, Taoist, Buddhist, and even Occidental philosophical tradition, while the grammatical texture seems comparatively insignificant.

Japanese philosophy cannot be separated from the aesthetic evaluation of words. The Japanese reader sees the concept as an image. Therefore, characters written by a master are pictures, works of art, and are appreciated as such[1]. Not only is the brush-work important, but also the character that has been chosen by the writer. A sequence of characters can have much meaning for the Japanese reader, whereas the translation seems to transmit no progression in thought. Except in a few cases of linguistic creations such as Fichte's "Tathandlung" and Hegel's "Aufheben", we are not inclined to consider the choice of words a philosophical accomplishment.

But Nishida's philosophy is abundant in word-creations and new character-compounds. Due to the nature of the Chinese characters, compounds are an enrichment of meaning, whereas in western languages an accumula-

---

1) See the reproduction of Nishida's handwriting on the frontispiece. This shows a poem in the form of a scroll (kakemono).

tion of words tends to have the opposite effect. For
this reason we translate the baroque-sounding title
"Absolutely contradictory self-identity" ("Zettai mujunteki jikodōitsu") simply as "Oneness of opposites". And
such a difficult compound as "hyôgen-saiyô-teki", literally
"expression-activity-like", had to be translated sometimes
as "expressive" and sometimes as "through the function
of expression"; for us the word "expression" (Ausdruck)
loses its original significance and depth through its com-
bination with "activity".

The aesthetic value of words lies, among other things,
in the richness and variety of their possible meanings.
The poet's word appeals to the free imagination and does
not want to be restricted to one single, clearly defined
meaning. In this regard, the Japanese language is
poetical by nature. This advantage, however, becomes
a disadvantage in science, where logical expression is
necessary. When, in Japanese, a character (representing
the subject of a phrase) is defined by another, synonymous
character (representing the predicate) it may sound
very profound in Japanese; the translation, however, turns
out to be mere tautology. In Japanese, the progression
of thought goes from image to image, from emotion to
emotion, and therefore loses in translation much more
of its original richness than a translation from one
occidental language into another. Taking into consideration all these factors, it may be said that due to the
different language and the different way of thinking
and expressing oneself, comprehension of Japanese
philosophy through the medium of translation is very

difficult, though not impossible. In general it may be stated that Japanese thinking has the form of totality (Ganzheit): starting from the indistinct total aspect of a problem, Japanese thought proceeds to a more distinct total grasp by which the relationship of all parts becomes intuitively clear. This way of thinking is intuitive and directed rather by mood, atmosphere, and emotion, than by mere calculating intellect. To start from one part and consider its relations to the other parts and to the architectural structure of the whole, appears very abstract to the Japanese mind. Moreover, politeness will not allow of his calling things too directly by name. The Japanese language is slightly evasive and little concerned with detail. Occidental evolution of mind, it may be said, goes in the opposite direction: modern thought tries to escape from all too differentiated and analytical methods, striving for some sort of integrated thinking. On the contrary, the Japanese tries to escape from all too undifferentiated and integrated methods, seeking in Western philosophy logic and analysis. All the difficulties mentioned above are still further increased when we deal with problems which in themselves touch the inexpressible, as in the case of Nishida's philosophy. Before dealing with his philosophy, however, we should survey the cultural background of his and the rest of Japanese philosophy.

CHAPTER 2

The Historical Background of Modern Japanese Philosophy

The Japanese philosophy of life in general rests on a threefold basis: First, there is a genuine respect for the past, which is the essence of "Shinto" (i.e. The Way of the Gods), the archaic, indigenous religious cult of Japan. Second, introduced from China, there is the Confucian moral order of society with emphasis on the present. Third, there is Buddhism with its emphasis on the future and eternity, introduced from India via China and Korea. In ancient times the soul of Japan found its expression in Shinto. For over two thousand years this mythical expression of the deepest self of the Japanese people has preserved itself with undiminished directness, and reaches into modern life, like a stratum of ancient rocks, together with later layers of reflective and sophisticated consciousness. Shinto represents the rhythm of life of the Japanese people as a social and racial whole, and encompasses all phases of communal activity. It received visible form as mythology and as a "national cult", but lives invisibly and formlessly in the hearts of

7

every individual. Shinto is the consciousness of the national hearth, of "Nippon" as eternal home and holy order. Outside of Japan the individual always feels lonely and lost. In Shinto there is a feeling that nature (which according to the cosmogonical myths was not made but begotten) is sacred and pure. This feeling is expressed in the veneration of mountains, waterfalls and trees, as well as in the pure and simple architecture of the central Shinto shrine at Ise. The old Japanese State philosophy was based on the concept of "kokutai" (land-body) which means the consciousness of the unity and natural sacredness of the country. In the new constitution the emperor, though having no political function, still represents the nation. A fundamental feature of all Japanese philosophy is the respect for nature as something sacred, pure, and complete in itself. Above all, Shinto means reverence for the imperial and familial ancestors. We might even speak of a communion between the living and the dead,— an eternal presence of the past.

In contrast to this deep-rooted emotional trend in Japanese life, Confucianism forms a rational and sober moral code of social behaviour. Confucian ethics formed the solid structure of Japanese society in olden days and, despite modernization, even today. This system of clearly defined duties is like a later rationalization of the early emotional ties in family and state. Confucian ethics consist of the following five relationships: Emperor-subject, father-son, older brother-younger brother, man and wife, friend and friend. Around this fundamental structure, we find woven a wealth of practical rules of etiquette and customs. The conviction that there is a correlation between the outward forms of social behavior and the inward form of character, lies at the base of Confucian philosophy. From this root springs a strong desire for form and distinct delimitation. It is here that the family system which is the lasting foundation of Japanese communal life, finds its moral justification. Here all duties are clearly defined and delimited. Such delimitation and classification, however, can become a danger to the living natural unity: the danger of overspecialization, bureaucracy, and inflexibility. With regard to philosophy, it is thanks to Confucianism that, in Japan, a philosopher is not only judged by his intellectual achievements but—perhaps primarily — by his personality. Therefore he, as the master, commands the same respect as the father or elder brother. Throughout his life he remains the teacher, the master, the "sensei" (i.e. teacher in the Japanese sense of the word). Respect for the master always controls the critical mind of the disciple, and subdues his strong desire for individuality and originality. The critical, dismissive gesture, so much liked by young Western thinkers, has never been considered good taste in the East.

While Shintoism means the eternal presence of the past, and Confucianism the practical, moral shaping of the present, Buddhism opens the gates to the eternal future. Japanese philosophy, which has kept aloof from the dogmatism of Buddhist sects, is yet inseparable from the spiritual atmosphere of Buddhism. As Mahayana

Buddhism, it has dominated Japanese minds and has ruled intellectual life for 1500 years. Mahayana Buddhism is basically pantheistic; its prevailing idea is that Buddha is in all things, and that all things have Buddha-nature. All things, all beings are potentially predestined to become Buddha, to reach salvation.

To comprehend the Buddha-nature in all things, an approach is required which ignores the peculiarities of things, and experiences absolute oneness. When the peculiarity and individuality of all things, and also of the human ego disappear, then, in absolute emptiness, in "nothingness", appears absolute oneness. By meditative submersion into emptiness, space, nothingness, such revelation of the oneness of all beings brings about absolute peace of mind and salvation from suffering.

"Nirvana", popularly considered a paradise after death, is but the realization of such experience of absolute oneness. In this experience, the soul, as the old German mystics say, is submerged in the infinite ocean of God. However, Buddhism does not use the word God or deity and knows no individual soul. The various sects differ in their methods of reaching salvation: in one sect, for instance, the mere invocation of Buddha's name suffices, if it is done sincerely and continuously.[1] More philosophical sects, however, require special methodical practices of meditation, in order to experience absolute oneness and thus achieve salvation.

Recalling what was said above about the unity and

---

1) See: D.T. Suzuki "Essays in Zen-Buddhism", Vol. II p. 179 ff.

sacredness of nature in Shintoism, it can be understood why Mahayana Buddhism with its pantheistic trend could take root in Japan, and live for so many centuries in perfect harmony or even symbiosis with Shintoism. Although during the Meiji revolution, Shintoism was restored as an independent cult, Buddhism and Shintoism still live in peaceful coexistence in the Japanese heart.

In contrast to the early Indian form of Hinayana Buddhism, Mahayana Buddhism considers itself neither pessimistic nor hostile toward nature and life. Again and again Japanese Buddhists affirm that Buddhism is not negative but positive. This is to be taken in the pantheistic sense of Mahayana Buddhism. Even the fundamental concept of "MU" (Nothingness) receives a positive meaning through the doctrine of the identity of the one with the many. The Buddhists use the word "soku" which means "namely", and say: "the world is one, namely many". The enlightened recognizes Samsara as Nirvana.

A significant difference between Hinayana and Mahayana lies furthermore in the fact that the ideal "Arhat" desires to enter Nirvana and to become Buddha, i.e. enlightened, while in Mahayana Buddhism the "Bodhisattva" postpones his entering Nirvana, until all other living beings are saved. Therefore, Mahayana Buddhists offer prayers to the Saviour-Bodhisattva Amida. We may say, therefore, that Mahayana Buddhism with its idea of salvation by a saviour is essentially religious, while Hinayana Buddhism with its idea of self-salvation is comparatively non-religious. This clear distinction, how-

11

ever, does not prevent Mahayana Buddhists from absorbing Hinayana ideas, saying that self-salvation is identical with salvation by a saviour "jiriki soku tariki": (own power namely other power).

The early, pessimistic Buddhism, as it was introduced to us by Schopenhauer, was transformed into the pantheistic Mahayana Buddhism which came to China and then to Japan.[1]

Of all Buddhist sects and schools in Japan, "Zen", which Ohasama[2] calls the "living Buddhism of Japan", is philosophically the most important. Even today, it is hard to estimate how much Japanese culture owes to the influence of Zen Buddhism since the Kamakura Period (13th century).[3] Zen is not a philosophy in the academic sense of the word. Other Buddhist schools,

---

1) In spite of the positive meaning of Mahayana Buddhism, we must hold Buddhism responsible for the obvious melancholic and resigned atmosphere of Japanese literature. Western observers stress the melancholic mood in the aesthetic categories such as "mono-no-aware", "yûgen", and "sabi". Japanese writers, however, stress the worldliness and the satisfaction in sensual phenomena, as seen in the Ukiyoe. Thus we may say that the Japanese are more conscious of their original, pre-Buddhist, worldly nature, while the western observer is more conscious of the later layers of Buddhist religion and Confucian morals.

2) Ohasama-Faust, Zen, the living buddhism in Japan, "Zen, der lebendige Buddhismus in Japan", Gotha-Stuttgart 1925.

3) D. T. Suzuki "Zen and its Influence on Japanese Culture". Suzuki attributes to Zen Buddhism an all-encompassing influence on Japanese culture and regards it as an essential element in the development of the Japanese character. Others, however, regard Zen as an alien influence and not essentially Japanese. This controversy reflects the complexity of the historical phenomenon that a nation discovers its own essence in the mirror of an alien culture.

such as Kegon and Tendai, are much richer in logical subtleties and metaphysical speculation. In some respects, Zen is more comparable to mediaeval German Mysticism. There are, however, essential differences with which we shall deal later on.

What is Zen, and what is it not? Certainly it is not a theory; this is the very point in which Zen differs from philosophy which seeks theoretical knowledge. For the same reason, Zen is not Theology; in contrast to a religion based on theology and history, Zen is a living practice based on the desire for salvation.

Zen is essentially non-rational, and, in this respect, it resembles mysticism; its basis is not a dogma, but an immediate and, therefore, inexpressible experience. When Zen speaks, the speech is inevitably indirect, circumscriptive and suggestive, and it indicates a singularly individual and personal religious or metaphysical experience. The goal of this experience is enlightenment, its fulfillment Nirvana. Enlightenment takes place suddenly, as with a stroke of lightening; in Japanese this is called "satori". Therefore, such indirect statements by Zen Buddhists are mostly paradoxical. The statement wants to express something which is essentially inexpressible. The paradox is equally important in German mysticism. That leads to the thought that Hegel's dialectical method is, to a great extent, of mystical heritage. In Japanese philosophy, especially in Nishida's philosophy, we find paradox and dialectical logics. This is not mere outward acceptance of Eckhart's mysticism, Hegel's dialectics, and Kierkegaard's paradox; it is an

13

inward grasping of problems which arise from original Zen experiences. Upon later reflection, this original experience is related to Western philosophy.

What separates Zen from Christian mysticism, is its worldliness and its practical tendency. Zen Buddhism developed historically from fantastical speculation in India to sober practicality in China, with the rejection of all magic. In Japan, this metamorphosis has been completed with a tendency towards simplicity and essentiality. This explains why Zen came to be an important factor in the education of the Japanese "bushi" (knight), and is still highly esteemed as an educational method for building the character through concentration. The artistic development and character-shaping of the Japanese personality in reference to "Ganzheit" and completeness of existence, no doubt owes a great deal to the influence of Zen.

Still we do not know what Zen really is. In order to find it out we should perhaps go to a Zen Monastery ourselves, and take part in the meditative practice under the leadership of an experienced monk. This activity is called "Zazen" which, in practice and in name, goes back to Indian "Dhyana". Even if, after months or years of practice, we should finally reach "satori", i.e. enlightenment, we should not be able to express it in words, because the essential experience remains inexpressible. The principle of Zen is silence. Only the experienced Zen-master is able to recognize without rational communication one who has been transformed by satori. Enlightenment is not so much an intellectual process, as a complete transformation of man. It is, as our mystics say, death and rebirth.[1]

With a man's transformation, the whole world is seen in a new light. That is because he himself has turned peaceful, strong and serene from within. The rhythm of life has changed. Meister Eckhart said that neither love, nor sorrow, nor anything created by God in time, could destroy him, who has experienced the birth of God within himself, and that all things appear insignificant and ineffective to him. Equally decisive, though less heartfelt, sometimes even rough in its outward expression, is the transformation by "satori"[2].

According to all indirect indications from Zen writers, "satori" means the discovery of the Buddha-nature of the universe within one's own heart. It is the gate leading directly to one's heart, and to the possibility of becoming Buddha, by introspection into one's own essence.[3]

According to the general doctrine of Mahayana Buddhism, the divine centre of Being is "Dharmahaya" which is one and the same in all beings. Being is one as well as many. The One is the essence, the Many are the multiplicity of phenomena. Just as the Christian mystic sees God in all things, the Mahayana Buddhist sees "Dharmahaya" in all things. The symbol of the mirror or "mirroring", so well known to Christian mystics, is also used by Buddhists to explain the reflection of

---

1) See page 137, the Zen poem quoted by Nishida.
2) See the many Zen legends as told by Ohasama and Suzuki.
3) Kitabatake Chikafusa "Shinnoshotoki" translated into German by H. Bohner, Tokyo 1935 Vol. I p. 264.

Dharmahaya in all things. This same concept of "reflecting" is a fundamental concept in Nishida's philosophy. Buddhists say that Dharmahaya is in all things, in the same way as the one and undivided moon is reflected in water, in the ocean as well as in millions of dewdrops, or even in dirty puddles. In each reflection the moon is whole and undivided. A heart which is torn by passions is too dull a mirror to reflect Dharmahaya. Therefore meditation is necessary to empty and purify the soul.

When enlightened by "satori", the soul becomes transparent.[1] All things, too, of a sudden, obtain a crystal-like transparency. The divine depth of all Being shines through all beings. Judging by all that has been said about Zen, everything depends on whether or not one can bring about a revelation of the essence of Being in one's own existence. Heideggers words about the revelation of Being in human existence through "Nothing" appear familiar to Japanese thinkers. Once man has reached the transcendent and transcendental unity, he has surpassed all antithetic opposites. Even the fundamental opposition of knowing subject and known object, has disappeared; this means knowledge has turned into being, or existence. The enlightened one does not comprehend Buddha, but becomes Buddha.

Zen emphasizes that Gautama achieved enlightenment under the Bodhi-tree and thus became Buddha, i.e. enlightened. Therefore, Zen considers enlightenment

---

1) See the reports on experiences given in Suzuki's "Essays" Vol. II.

the essence of Buddhism. Enlightenment itself means entering Nirvana. Disregarding all dogmatic doctrines and claiming "direct" tradition, Zen strives vigorously toward this goal of enlightenment. The practice of meditation which has been developed over the centuries serves this goal. The sermon merely prepares the mind, and "ko-an", the paradoxical problem for meditation, is meant to break down the intellect. All this has value only as a medium to clear the way for intuition; it is meant only to help to open the door from within. For the enlightened one who sees Buddha in himself and in all things, a stone is more than a stone. There is a famous garden in Kyoto consisting of nothing but stones and sand. The stones are often compared with tigers and lions. But they are more than stones, not because they resemble tigers or other things, but because they are stones through and through, and are as such an outward form of pure reality. Using Christian mystic symbolism we may say that the enlightened sees the eye of God in a delicately opened lotus blossom; and the same eye of God shines from the enlightened one. Meister Eckhart says "the eye with which I see God, is the same eye with which God sees me". Of course, Mahayana Buddhists do not speak of God, but of Nothingness.

From such grasping of the final unity in nothingness, springs assurance and relaxation of our existence. Warriors enter battle, saints live in the loneliness of woods, painters draw a spiritualized landscape with a few sure strokes of the brush so that even stones come to life. Buddha is in all things.

17

Zen means a full life. Every moment of our human existence can be decisive and can become the self-revelation of reality: a quiet moment of contemplation in a tiny tea pavillion, a fine autumn rain outside, the picture in the alcove showing two vigorously drawn Chinese characters "Lion Roars". Reality in its full vigour is completely and undividedly present in this quiet moment of contemplation.

Zen means concentrated but flexible force, an inwardly rich life, existence from the centre, completely balanced freedom at every moment.

Does this not mean that Zen is everything? Is this not the goal of every true and practical philosophy? Zen does not strive for the glory of originality in setting this goal; Zen is practice on the way to this goal. If we can say, for instance, that Goethe lived such a full life from the centre, he had, as the Zen Buddhists would say, Zen. Perhaps this is the reason why the Japanese have a strong and genuine interest in Goethe.[1]

Let us ask the opposite question, what is not Goethe in Zen seen from our point of view? First of all, there is the non-existence of the ego. Though Goethe, in his old age, had the wisdom of resignation, this never reached the degree of oriental depersonalization (Entpersönlichung). We in the West are separated from the East by our high esteem of the individual soul, original personality, and genius. Secondly, there is the limitation of the monastery walls and the meditation facing a rock. This

1) See: Nishida "Goethe's Metaphysical Background" in this book.

contradicts our concept of a full life. Of course Zen, too, emphasizes its practice in daily life, but there is always a note of asceticism in it. Our concept of a full life, on the other hand, goes back to Greek art and Roman politics, mediaeval Christianity and Faustian drive, the Italian Renaissance and German romanticism. Since, however, Nothingness plays an important role in Christian mysticism, it is not absolutely certain that the impersonal concept of Buddhist "Dharmahaya" is altogether incompatible with Western thought.

One thing is important: Zen is not content to "know" what we have called a "full life", but puts all its effort into living it, into literally" "grasping" it. One cannot grasp the unity of life by learning and knowing, but only by practising. Only from within, from the middle (which is not localized in the head, but in the "Tanden", the centre of gravity of the body), flows the vigorous, quiet force of the painter's brush and the warrior's sword. Tension and uncertainty are inevitable as long as the head, the intellect, the self-conscious mind is fixed on something or the negation of something.[1]

According to Suzuki complete intellectual relaxation

It is noteworthy that a Japanese psychiatrist is successfully letting his patients practice Zen-meditation, instead of psychoanalyzing them. In this connection C. G. Jung's introduction to a German translation of Suzuki's essays "Die Grosse Befreiung", Leipzig 1939, is of special interest. Jung emphasizes the importance of the subconscious and natural elements in Zen which are generally the basis of religion. However, he perhaps overemphasizes the objective images at the expense of the subjective behaviour of the subconscious "élan vital", which is the result of Zen discipline.

and emptiness set free the energy which is guided by the flow of reality itself and brings about absolute freedom. Absolute nothingness and emptiness allow a somnambulistic certainty and sureness. It is through Nothingness that Zen finds the fullness of life.

CHAPTER 3

Nishida as The Representative
Philosopher of Modern Japan

It has been shown above how Japanese life is based on Shintoism, Confucianism (including Taoism), and Buddhism. They all have one thing in common; practicality out-weighs the theoretical element, and is verified by the wholeness (Ganzheit) and completeness of human existence. At once, thinker, poet, painter, and master of the sword, the Japanese desires existential mastery in his contact with the world. He wants to "grasp" life. This may be the reason why the soul of Japan did not seek adequate expression in theoretical philosophy, but preferred art as a means of expressing its innermost self.

Philosophy in its narrow, academic sense, does not appear in Japan until the Meiji-Era. Yet, letters written by Jesuit missionaries of the 16th century show that Buddhists, especially Zen-Buddhists equalled their Western opponents in philosophical disputation, or at least made it very difficult for them.[1]

All the values of European civilization opened up before the Japanese mind during the Meiji-Era, and did so all at once. The Japanese were caught in a tremendous surge, much as had been the case in Europe at the time of the Renaissance.

Philosophy in the Western sense of the word, was first introduced into Japan during this Meiji Period, and received the name of "tetsu-gaku" (i.e. science of wisdom). Under this name philosophy became a special course at the newly founded Imperial University in Tokyo. A German philosopher, Dr. R. Köber, a pupil of Eucken, was invited to Tokyo and he introduced German classical idealism. His name and his work are still unforgotten among the old generation of Japanese scholars.

These were the "Lehrjahre" of Japanese philosophy. Three schools gained influence:

1. German idealism, particularly Fichte. His philosophy of "Tathandlung" was apparently congenial to the heroic impulses of the Meiji Period.

2. American pragmatism, whose anti-speculative common-sense philosophy appealed to the Japanese in their inclination toward immediate practicality.

3. Bergson's irrationalistic philosophy of the "élan vital" which had a special appeal to Japan's feeling for

---

1) See: Georg Schurhammer, S. J., "Die Disputationen des P. Cosme de Torres S. J. mit den Buddhisten in Yamaguchi im Jahre 1551", Mitteilungen der O.A.G. Tokyo 1929.

life and nature.[1]   There seems to be a close inner relationship with the threefold basis of Japanese philosophy which has been discussed earlier.

Japan's "Wanderjahre", when Japanese scholars were sent abroad by the government to study in many lands, seem to be over.   Japanese philosophers are trying to reconcile what is general in philosophy with the specific metalogical prerequisites of Japanese thinking.   Thus Japanese philosophy hopes to do justice to the general logical postulates as well as to its own historically conditioned peculiarities.   The representative of modern Japanese philosophy is, in this sense, Kitaro Nishida.

Nishida was born in the revolutionary Meiji period and died in 1945.   His philosophical activity as teacher and writer filled the first half of our century, and made him the venerated master of Japanese philosophy.   There is no philosopher in Japan today who was not influenced by him.   When Nishida retired from his post at Kyoto University in 1928, his follower Gen Tanabe succeeded him and kept up the fame of the philosophical faculty of that university.   Now Tanabe too, has retired and lives in the mountains, writing books which bring back to life Buddhist thinking by relating it to existentialism and dialectical theology.[2]

The collected works of Kitaro Nishida have appeared

---

1) See: G. Kuwaki "Die philosophischen Tendenzen in Japan", Kant-studien 1928.
2) See: Taketi "Die japanische Philosophie" in "Blätter für deutsche Philosophie", 1940.

in 14 volumes published by Iwanami, Tokyo. The following are the English titles of these volumes in chronological order.

 I. "A Study of the Good".

 II. "Thought and Experience".

 III. "Intuition and Reflection in the Consciousness of the Self".

 IV. "The Problem of the Consciousness of the Self".

 V. "Art and Ethics".

 VI. "From Causing to Seeing".

 VII. "Self-consciousness of the Universal" (This volume contains among others the essay "The Intelligible World" which is translated in this book.)

 VIII. "Self-Determination of Nothingness".

 IX. "Fundamental Problems of Philosophy"—"The World of Action".

 X. "Fundamental Problems. New series".—"The Dialectical World".

 XI. "Collection of Philosophical Essays—Outline of a System of Philosophy".

 XII. "Thought and Experience. New Series". (This volume contains the essay "Goethe's Metaphysical Background" which is translated in this book.)

 XIII. "Collection of Philosophical Essays. Second Series."

 XIV. "Collection of Philosophical Essays. Third Series" (This volume contains the essay "Unity of Opposites" which is translated in this book.)

In foreign translation the following have appeared: in German, translated by F. Takahashi: "Die morgenländischen und abendländischen Kulturformen in alter Zeit, vom metaphysischen Standpunkte aus gesehen" (in den Abhandlungen der Preussischen Akademie der Wissenschaften, 1939) and "Die Einheit des Wahren,

Guten und Schönen" (in Journal of the Sendai International Society 1940).

This book gives an English version of three essays which have appeared in German translation: Kitaro Nishida "Die intelligible Welt" Walter de Gruyter, Berlin, 1943.

Nishida's philosophy, no matter how much influenced by Western thinking, has its roots in his own existence and returns to it. The oriental and particularly Japanese element of his character is shown in the way he handles the philosophical problems so familiar to the West. Of course his thinking has gone through many changes during the long period of his life. However, these changes are in a way consistent. This becomes evident in the relationship between the three essays translated in this book.

Nishida's method can be called indicative, and penetrates more and more into the depth of consciousness. (Consciousness itself is activated and kept in motion by dialectical contradictions). That, which is first seen as from afar, becomes clearer and clearer during the process of his thinking. This method may be called indicative because new and more distinct visions open up to the penetrating eye. His essays could also be called meditations. Nishida seems to develop his thoughts in the process of writing, and to write in the process of thinking. He does not place a finished thought before us. That is why the reader must follow the spirals of his thinking. The reader must actually think along with him.

In order to understand Nishida, we must remember

what has been said above about Japanese philosophy in general and Zen-Buddhism in particular. Nishida was greatly influenced by Zen. In his method the preference for the paradox and dialectical thinking stems from Zen. In his style, the frequent repetitions, which are like magic invocations, also stem from Zen.

Above all, it is the content of his philosophy which is related to Zen mysticism as well as to Christian mysticism. Many basic thoughts, it is true, have been taken from German Idealism and from Dilthey. However, if an attempt were made to trace all the influences with philological preciseness, it would miss the essential point, because the essential is always the whole and not the details. The fact that he shares many thoughts with other thinkers, does not speak against his philosophy since philosophy prefers truth to originality. The whole of his philosophy culminates in the concept of the Nothingness of Buddhist metaphysics. All things and even thinking itself, are an explication or unfolding of Nothingness.

Nishida's great influence is, to some extent, due to the fact that his personality itself made a lasting impression on the minds of his pupils. The Japanese sense strongly whether the whole person philosophizes or merely the intellect. Western philosophers who found the way back from intellectual virtuosity to existential philosophy, will understand this point very well. Unfortunately a translation of philosophical texts cannot transmit an impression of the personality. For this reason a handwritten poem by Nishida appears reproduced on the front page.

Its translation is as follows:

The bottom of my soul has such depth;
Neither joy nor the waves of sorrow can reach it.

CHAPTER 4

Being and Nothingness

Introduction to "The Intelligible World"

To be or not to be, has always been the fundamental question of philosophy. The occidental concept of absolute being, and the oriental concept of absolute nothingness, are the central problem of Nishida's essay "The Intelligible World".

"Intelligible world" is the translation of the Latin "mundus intelligibilis", and refers to the Platonic world of ideas. Truth, beauty, and the good have their logical "place" in the intelligible world. These ideas, having the character of norms or values, may be called "ideal beings".

"Real beings", as they are usually called, like anorganic, organic, and living beings, have their place in the natural world.

The psychological phenomena require categories of their own, and belong to the world of inner perception, or the world of self-consciousness.

Nishida, therefore, defines three spheres of "being", and three "worlds": the natural world, the world of consciousness, and the intelligible world. Their definition and interrelation are the theme of this essay.

Every "being" is determined. Is it determined by another being? What is the last by which everything is determined?

"Nothingness" is the transcendental and transcendent unity of opposites. The last enveloping to which our thinking, feeling, and acting self penetrates, in which all contradictions have been resolved, and in which the abyss between the thinking subject and the thought object disappears, in which even the opposite position of God and soul no longer exists—this last in which every being has its "place" and is thereby defined as being, cannot itself be defined as being, and does not have its "place" in anything else; therefore it is called non-being, or Nothingness. Nothingness is the transcendental and transcendent unity of opposites. Here the soul in its greatest depth, is a clear mirror of eternity.

Nishida does not try to deduce dogmatically from this concept of nothingness all defined being, such as form, temporality, individuality and personality. On the contrary, he tries to show and indicate how all defined being, such as form temporality, individuality, and personality, in the end stand in this "nothingness" and are enveloped by "nothingness". He tries to show how "nothingness" is that last which forms the background for everything. Nishida does not try to define the indefinable, and to perceive transcendence metaphysically. But he wants to indicate or point to transcendence in and behind everything. (We are here reminded of

30

Jaspers' concept of metaphysics). To have transcendence reveal itself, is not an epistemological definition, nor is it scientific knowledge of transcendence.

"Being" means "to be determined". That which determines is the "universal". According to Hegel, the logical judgement has the following form: "the individual is the universal". The individual being is determined as such by concepts and universal ideas. From the point of view of logic, an individual being is defined by a complexity of ideas. Since knowledge is achieved through logical judgements, Nishida calls it "self-determination of the 'universal'". The one who makes the judgement, is of no relevance to the meaning and the truth of the judgement.

In the "universal of judgement", the reality of nature is defined and determined as "being". Nishida says the world of nature has its "place" in the "universal of judgement". Being is always being "within". Therefore the meaning of different worlds of being, or realms of being, is defined and determined by the specific "being within", and by the specific "universal" which is its "place" or field.

First, there is the "natural world", the world of outward experience, the physical universe. This world has its "place" in the "universal of judgement". In the predicative dimension, in the "plan of predicates", are the predicates which determine an individual subject which can never become a predicate itself.

Second, there is the world of inner experience, the "world of consciousness". "Being" means, in this second

31

world, being within consciousness. Here the "universal" is the "universal of self-consciousness". The outward world is, metaphorically speaking, "lined" with this inward world, just as a good Japanese kimono is lined with precious silk. This second realm of being is deeper and at the same time higher, it is "enveloping". But as long as our consciousness merely knows its content, this content is still somewhat alien. Only through will and action does our consciousness make its content its own. The acting ego makes the external world its sphere of action. Action, being an occurrence in the outward world, is at the same time "expression" of the will. The outward is the expression of the inward; the acting self makes the outward world a part of itself. The outward world is enveloped by the ego in the same way as the inward world. In the realm of the willing and acting self, the "universal of self-consciousness" becomes truly enveloping. Emotion is the union of the subject and the object, of outward and inward.

Third, there is the "intelligible world", Plato's world of ideas. Here the "universal" is no longer the "universal of judgement" nor the "universal of self-consciousness", but the "universal of intellectual intuition" or the "intelligible universal". We have seen that in the "universal of judgement" the subject is determined by predicates; in the "universal of self-consciousness" the self determines itself; in the "intelligible universal" the transcendental self is determined by intellectual intuition, in the perception of the "idea". The ideas of the True, the Good, and the Beautiful form the content of the "intelligible world". Thus we have three layers of being: natural being, conscious being, and intelligible being. We reach each higher, deeper level by "transcending" the former level of being. By transcending the plane of the predicates, the predicating self appears on the horizon of the predicates; it is the subject of the world of self-consciousness. In the other direction, namely in the direction of the logical subject of the judgement, the irrationality of the individual being reaches beyond the "natural world". In the world of consciousness we no longer have subject and predicate confronting each other, but self and content. But there is a new contradiction which again necessitates the act of transcendence. The self, as willing self, contains the contradiction that it simultaneously affirms and negates the non-ego. This contradiction leads to a new "transcending" from the world of self-consciousness into the realm of the transcendental, the world of Kant's "Bewusstsein überhaupt". At the same time the content of consciousness reaches beyond itself into the transcendental world of ideas. In the depth of our personal self is the transcendental self which sees itself intuitively. This self-contemplation contains "ideas" in the Platonic sense of the word. Within this intellectual intuition, greatest harmony is achieved in the aesthetic intuition; here, inward and outward are identical.

Seen from the point of view of consciousness, aesthetic intuition is creative in the highest sense of the word. However, the general consciousness ("Bewusstsein überhaupt") is creative in other directions, too. As pure

FERNALD LIBRARY
COLBY-SAWYER COLLEG
NEW LONDON, N.H. 0325

85320

subject of knowledge, it contains the realm of constitutive categories with which it constructs the object of knowledge in judgements. Still, it is the real world which, in the end, forms the content of this theoretical intellectual intuition. Such theoretical intuition is merely formal, and demonstrates only the abstract side of the idea. Therefore the meaning of the real world has changed, and the "consciousness-in-general" confronts a world of values and meanings.

The object-character is completely lost in moral consciousness; here the "general consciousness" contemplates upon the idea of the good; there is a world of values, and a world of law; all object-character disappears. The intelligible self directly sees itself in its conscience. The idea of the good is regulative and no longer intuitively visible, like the idea of the Beautiful which is the revelation of eternity.

Nishida tries to comprehend the "consciousness-in-general" as "being", by giving it its "place". On the other hand he relates the "general consciousness" to our individual consciousness by recognizing the "intellectual self" as the core of our personal and individual self. This core becomes apparent when the problems of the willing ego press to transcend it; the willing ego itself transcends into the "intelligible universal", where ego and non-ego are reconciled by "intellectual intuition". The "intelligible world" is not another world, a world of transcendence, but the innermost centre of our real world.

Within the intelligible self, the moral self has reached

34

pure self-intuition in its conscience. But even the conscience still contains a contradiction: the more moral, the more immoral it is. Partly in the sense of moral pride (the sinner is nearest to God), partly because we feel the more guilty the stronger our conscience speaks. Therefore even the moral consciousness transcends itself towards absolute transcendence. "Even the idea of the good is the shadow of something which, in itself, has no form" (Nishida). By transcending the sphere of morality we reach the sphere of religion. In this very depth of the self there is a "negation of self". Without such self-negation there is no "life in God". Christian Platonists said that the Platonic ideas have their place in God. But Nishida thinks that Zen Buddhism, with its concept of nothingness, reaches further than the Christian religion. The "last enveloping universal", in which all being has its place and is thereby defined as being, cannot by itself be defined as being; it is merely "place" and "nothingness".

Where we are open to this nothingness, there, and only there, is "being" revealed. We remember that Heidegger said that Being is evident when it is held in nothingness. ("Ins Nichts gehalten wird das Sein offenbar.")

The essence of Leibniz's theodicy is that light becomes evident only in contrast with dark. Malebranche's metaphysics differs from this in that he wants to paint a picture on a golden background like a Gothic painting without shadows; Nishida's nothingness, we might say, is both darkness and golden background. And in front

35

of this eternal background, all being is as it is, without "whence" or "whither". Being is there with "wonderful self-identity". Such an affirmation of being is a kind of salvation, and does not stem from moral consciousness with its contradictions, but from a depth where good and evil no longer exist. Here the religious consciousness discovers "nothingness".

Nishida's concept of nothingness (mu), and the Christian mystical concept of nothingness (Nichts), have in common the idea that nothingness transcends not only the sphere of opposites, but all objectivity, and still remains the basis of all objectivity and being. Eckhart's concept of nothingness means that God is not a definable being, but the basis of all definable being. Nishida, however, does not allow any interpretation of nothingness whatever. Western metaphysics are fundamentally ontological, Nishida's concept of nothingness does not allow any ontological interpretation such as Plato's "true being", or Hegel's "Geist", or Fichte's "tathandelndes Ich". It is just nothingness. Nishida's nothingness is not like Hegel's nothingness, which is but the antithesis to being; it is more like Hegel's "true infinite" ("gutes Unendliches") which is present in and with finite being. Nishida's pupil, Koyama, sees the peculiarity of Japanese thought in this very concept of nothingness, which is present in and with all being, therefore alive and fulfilled, while the Indian concept of nothingness is essentially emptied and other-worldly. According to Koyama, the doctrine of two worlds and the concept of transcendence (as another world) are alien to the Japanese mind.

In one respect, taken in the sense of transcendental idealism, nothingness is the basis of all definition and determination, and therefore itself not defined and not determined. In another respect it is the basis of everything personal, and therefore itself not personal. Again in another respect it is the basis of all being and therefore itself not a being, but nothingness.

Metaphysically speaking, all being is a self-unfolding of the eternal, formless nothingness; all finite forms are shadows of the formless. This is in a sense pantheism, since nothingness is present in all being as its deepest core, essentially impersonal, and never an object of knowledge. The transcendental and metaphysical aspects coincide when Nishida says that all being has its final "place" in nothingness.

"Place" is the central concept of Nishida's logic, and serves as a philosophical medium to treat uniformly intellectual knowledge, consciousness (in particular will and action), and religious experience. This basic philosophical concept of "place" applies equally to the "natural world", the "world of consciousness", and the "intelligible world". Nishida's idea was to replace Aristotle's "logics of the subject", where all predicates refer to a subject (Hypokeimenon) which remains as an irrational remnant, with his "logics of the predicate". In this "logics of place" (or field-logics) the subjects are determined by their "place". The "logical place" itself refers to the deeper layer where it has its place, and so forth, to the last "place", nothingness, which is the only irrational remnant. Nishida calls it the "universal

37

of absolute nothingness". Nishida departs from the object of knowledge which is represented in Logics by the subject of the judgement. He seeks the "place" in which and by which this object is defined and determined. When the nature of an object transcends the structural limits of the "place", when contradictions appear, a deeper layer of determination has to be sought, a more "enveloping universal", in which this object has its true "place", while the irrational remainder of this object in the former "place" disappears. Thus, by transcending one place, an "enveloping universal" becomes apparent. This "enveloping universal" is increasingly "concrete" compared with the first abstract "universal of judgement". The most concrete enveloping "place" is "nothingness".

By transcending in the direction of the object (subject of judgement—noema—intelligible noema) new worlds of objects (natural world—world of consciousness —intelligible world) become apparent as "being". At the same time this means transcending in the direction of the predicate (predicate of judgement—intention or noesis—intelligible noesis). This is a transcending of the self-conscious self. Being is always a "being in...", a "having its place". But that which is only place and does not have its place in something else, cannot be called "being". Therefore it is called "nothingness". There is a path leading from every "being" to "nothingness"; such being must be comprehended progressively as being determined by the "universal of judgement", and as being enveloped by the "universal of consciousness" and by the

38

"intelligible self" and by "nothingness". The intelligible self sees itself in the depth consciousness and is supported and enveloped by "nothingness". Splendour and fullness of being are infinitely intensified by the overwhelming realization that everything comes from "nothingness" and goes into "nothingness".

CHAPTER 5

Art and Metaphysics

Introduction to
"Goethe's Metaphysical Background"

According to Nishida, beauty is the appearance of eternity in time. At the same time art is "boundless unfolding of the free self". The idea of the beautiful is self-contemplation of the pure, intelligible self. This self-contemplation gains form in time, and this form belongs to reality which is at the same time subjective and objective. Subjective activity of the personality has the highest degree of objectivity when perfect harmony of the outward and inward has been achieved in a beautiful form, where the artist, in depicting the outward world, expresses his own self. This can be compared with mathematical truth, since a mathematical idea has objective truth to the degree to which it is pure and to which it is a spontaneous achievement of the personality, leaving behind so-called reality.

Pure subjectivity can realize itself only by penetrating into the objective world. Nishida says: "not until he stands before his canvas, brush in hand, can the painter find the way to his own infinite idea".[1]   Therefore, with regard to cultural activity in general, Nishida says: "The deeper the personality is, the more active it is".[2] This depth becomes apparent through activity.   Together with the concrete individual personality, that which stands behind it and "embraces it from behind", this depth reveals itself.[3]   This embracing or enveloping "last", which is the bottom of the intelligible self, is absolute "nothingness".   The beautiful is the revelation of the absolute through the medium of personality.

This "enveloping last" becomes perceivable as the metaphysical background of a piece of art.   To see a piece of art which is an expression of the artist's personality, is to perceive at the same time that which stands behind the artist.   Logical, rational thinking fails to determine that metaphysical background.   The only way is to perceive transcendence indirectly.   This extreme difficulty of expressing the inexpressible and of defining the indefinable explains the peculiarly indirect, subtle, and suggestive style of Nishida's, as it appears in his essay "Goethe's Metaphysical Background".   Indeed, the "metaphysical" in the title of the essay is not to be found in the original, but is added by the translator in order to avoid any misunderstanding of the word "background".   This addition is intended to suggest the breadth of thought and depth of feeling which is implied by Nishida in the

---

1) "The unity of the True, the Beautiful, and the Good" German translation by F. Takahashi, Sendai 1940, p. 131.
2) ibid., p. 132.
3) See: Nishida "Goethe's Metaphysical Background" in this book.

word "background" (haikei). As in a black and white painting of the Zen school, Nishida gives a few brush strokes which suggest what is to be read into his work. The essential elements remain incomprehensible as long as there is no creative cooperation on the part of the reader.

A piece of art, according to Nishida, is a relief cut out of the marble block of eternity. This block is an essential part and is not to be separated from the relief. Nishida feels strongly this background of eternity in Buddhist and early Christian art. Seeing those works, we are touched by the metaphysical vibration of the artist. The difference in art stems from the relationship of the background to that which is formed against it: Oriental art is essentially impersonal because the background is an integral part of it. This produces (in our hearts) a formless, boundless vibration, and an endless, voiceless echo".[1]

Greek art has a completely different "background". "Eternity in the Greek sense stands before us as something visible and does not embrance us from behind".[2] The Greek work of art is an image of the idea (platonic idea), its plastic beauty is perfect, but it still lacks a certain depth of background which appears later on in early Christian art. Early Christian art has "an inwardness which reminds us of Buddhist paintings in the East".[3] Typical historical changes of background have occurred.

---

1) Nishida "Goethe's metaphysical background". p. 146.
2) ibid., p. 146.
3) ibid., p. 146.

In the Renaissance the background corresponds to the forceful, vital, dynamic emotion of man in that period. In Michelangelo's art this background is "colossal...as if we stood in front of a deep crater's turbulent black flames".

In order to express the inexpressible and to define the indefinable, Nishida makes use of some concepts of Eastern art criticism. Such concepts are, for instance, "high-wide", "deep-wide", and "plane-wide", which characterize the inner width of a picture. In a similar way Nishida distinguishes "form" and "formlessness" in background. Form has either "height" (Dante) or "depth" (Michelangelo) formlessness has "height without height, depth without depth, or width without width". While the art of the Renaissance usually has form and height or form and depth in its background, Goethe's background is essentially formless, extending into infinity. However,—and this, according to Nishida, is characteristically German and Christian—, this background has something active and personal in it. "Goethe's concept of nature does not deny individuality; nature produces individual forms everywhere. Nature is like an infinite space which, though itself formless, produces form everywhere".[1] This formless, but form-creating background appears in Goethe's poetry as moonlight, as ocean, or as mist ("An den Mond", "Der Fischer", and "Erlkönig"). Everywhere this formlessness is personal, "it is essentially something that harmonizes with our

---

1) ibid.

soul".

Goethe's road, which leads from youthful Promethean Titanism to the resignation of old age, is interpreted by Nishida as the road from deed to salvation,—salvation which implies deed and endeavour (strebendes Bemühen). Here the personal is reconciled with the impersonal. "Goethe's monad differs from Leibniz' windowless monad in so far as it, resounding infinitely, fades away into the bottom of eternity." Nishida says that Goethe's concept of nature is formless but form-creating, and Nishida feels in this a kind of personal consonance, using the German word "Mitklingen". This consonance reaches "the unfathomable bottom of our soul." This means that the bottom of the soul and the bottom of the universe are one and the same, the "enveloping nothingness" of Nishida's philosophy. We are reminded of the unity of "Seelengrund" and "Grund der Gottheit" in Eckhart. Nishida finds in Goethe's metaphysical background "something like a friend's eye and like a friend's voice which comforts our soul."—"In Goethe there is no inward and outward; all that is, is as it is, comes from where there is nothing and goes where there is nothing; and just in this coming from nothingness and going into nothingness there is a gentle sound of humanity."

Life with this formless background of nothingness is itself by no means naught and empty. On the contrary it implies, as we have seen, personality, deed, and salvation; it is a full life to the highest degree. In this very existence Nishida sees the bridge to Eastern philosophy.

To Goethe, the man who sought liberation from Werther's sufferings, Rome gave the Roman Elegies; to the old Goethe who sought liberation from reality, the Orient gave the "West-Oestliche Divan"...."When we continue in this direction we touch upon something which is, like the art of the East, an art of sorrow without the shadow of sorrow, an art of joy without the shadow (and colour) of joy." This is the art of perfect peace of mind. The light of eternity is reflected in the bottom of the soul, like moonlight which shines undisturbed in the depth of a well.

Time and history are reconciled with eternity against that metaphysical background. Greek culture made everything an image of the idea, a "shadow of eternity"; its centre of gravity lies in the "eternal past." Christianity on the other hand makes everything a road to eternity; its centre of gravity lies in the "eternal future". The contradiction of these two points of view is dialectical, according to Nishida. The synthesis lies in a point of view which regards history not only as a stream flowing from eternal past to eternal future, but also as a "counter-flow against the movement from future to past." According to Nishida time is "quasi" born in eternal past and disappears in eternal future. But history is both: it is going with time and simultaneously is a continuous disappearing of the future in the past. It is as if we were ascending a descending escalator, so that the two movements counteract each other. We step into the future and the future approaches us, becomes present, and disappears in the past. We, however, are standing in the present

45

moment, in "the eternal now." History is a continual revolving movement in the eternal now. In this now, time is at once included and extinguished. Time and eternity are reconciled in the now.

In history, seen as temporality, enclosed by timeless nothingness, the personal is revealed as the content of eternity. Here time stands in eternity and eternity has entered time. "In the same way that our mind sees itself in itself, personality is an image of eternity which is reflected in eternity." This reflection takes place in the "eternal now"; "where time is included and at the same time extinguished, there the personal is seen as the content of eternity." This means: eternity and the personal are not to be sought in a transcendent world outside of history. Temporality enveloped by nothingness reveals the personal, and is itself a relief cut out of the marble of eternity. History is the self-determination of eternity in time, "self-limitation in eternal now." Goethe's metaphysical background, according to Nishida, points to this concept of history in which everything comes and goes from where there is nothing to where there is nothing, and everything is eternally what it is.

The encounter with transcendence goes through all forms of human existence as an eternal reverberation and resonance, and forms a specific rhythm of existence. Religion in this sense does not claim a field of its own and therefore does not collide with any other religion. It can be said that Shinto is the rhythm of Japanese life in state, community, and family, while Buddhism appeals to the individual and his metaphysical situation. In the

46

early days of Japanese history there were struggles for power between Shintoism and Buddhism; but later on they existed together in a kind of symbiosis, and today Shintoism which, by law, is considered a religion, lives side by side with Buddhism and is in no competition with it. To the degree to which it is still alive it is the natural rhythm of Japanese life.

Buddhism, too, seems to have lost the emphasis on its doctrine, and in the form of Zen Buddhism has become a special rhythm of life, not of national life, as in Shintoism, but of individual life. Moreover Japanese Buddhism has grown so far apart from early Indian Buddhism, that one is tempted to say that they have only their name in common. "Nothingness" in Nishida's philosophy comes from the Buddhist concept of nothingness and means the exact opposite of void and emptiness which mean nothingness in Indian Buddhism. Japanese Buddhism emphasizes the point that its nothingness is alive with infinite content, that it does not negate life. Nishida's philosophy is based on this positive Japanese philosophy of life and comprehends Being as self-unfolding of formless, eternal nothingness.

What has been said about Japanese philosophy, as represented by Nishida, requires supplementation. Nishida's meditation about Goethe's metaphysical background is more than a mere superficial synthesis of Western scientific philosophy and Eastern metaphysics; the very metaphysical basis of East and West is discussed. This discussion proves to be basically a common struggle with eternal problems of mankind, with the

47

silent understanding that the differences of nations do not negate the metaphysical unity of human existence.

This is not the place to define that unity of man's being; suffice it to mention the possibility of understanding alien civilizations. There must be a common ground of human experience where the philosophies of nations meet. That is why Christian mysticism has been quoted above for the purpose of comparison. The fundamental trend of mysticism which desires to overcome the contradiction of subject and object goes through all of Nishida's philosophy. In the "universal of intellectual intuition", by which the intelligible world is determined, idea as object and idea as vision coincide: "That which neutralizes intelligible noesis and intelligible noema in the universal of intellectual intuition, is that which sees itself." The intelligible self, seeing the idea of the beautiful, "forgets itself, loves the object as the self and unites with it."[1]

---

1) See: Nishida "The Intelligible World".

CHAPTER 6

Philosophy of History

Introduction to "The Unity of Opposites"

Nishida's philosophy seems to be extremely abstract. Still he opposes abstract logic. When the reader remembers that the Buddhist does not strive for knowing Buddha, but for becoming Buddha, and that Zen emphasizes the grasping of a full life by practice, he will understand how much Nishida must have been attracted by Hegel's concept of a "concrete logic" which tries to grasp reality in its dynamic historical unfolding. Abstract logic, on the contrary, is a timeless and spaceless projection of reality on an ideal screen or plane. Nishida tries to grasp reality with concrete dialectical logic.

Reality is material as well as spiritual. The natural world is comprehended by categories which allow the human mind to construct a model of matter and its mechanism. But for comprehending the historical world of human culture, other categories are required which allow to understand the struggle which is going on in man's mind. Man, formed by his environment under the spell of the past, is looking towards the future, trying to be creative, "forming", and free. This contradiction of past and future, or the struggle between environment and individual, takes place in man's mind and heart. It takes place here and now. This "Now" is the "one single present" in which past and future oppose and meet each other.

Wherever there is contradiction and struggle, there is reality. The world as a whole is always both sides of this contradicting and struggling reality, it is the "unity of opposites".

Faithful to the old Buddhist saying: "The willow is green, the flower is red"[1] Nishida, from the beginning, conceives reality as an inseparably interwoven unity of subjective and objective elements as unity of subject and object. "Everything that is regarded as being real, is subjective-objective. That which we perceive through our senses transcends our consciousness, but is, at the same time, our own sensation."[2] Most of all it is action which forms the centre of the subjective-objective world, because action is the expression of the subjective will, as well as an occurrence in the objective world. In a relatively early essay[3] Nishida calls the will "concrete reality". At that time he was mostly concerned with discovering the "essential content of personality in the core of objec-

---

1) Compare: "Die morgenländischen und abendländischen Kulturformen in alter Zeit vom metaphysischen Standpunkte aus gesehen"
   (transl. by F. Takahashi), Abhandlungen der Preussischen Akademie
   der Wissenschaften, Berlin 1939.
2) ibid.
3) "Die Einheit des Wahren, des Schönen und des Guten" (translated
   by F. Takahashi, Sendai 1940.)

tive knowledge". Knowledge, though focused on utilitarian and practical purposes, finally aims at a "renewal of personality." True reality is revealed in the depth of personality.

"True reality on the one hand forms a unity, on the other hand it is an eternal splitting up and eternal evolution. Reality contains endless contradictions which, however, form a unity. On the side of unity we find artistic intuition and on the side of division and evolution we find moral obligation..."[1] Here the emphasis lies on the subjective element as a transcendental apriori of objectivity. Later[2], Nishida defines reality as "self-unification" of subject and object. Finally, in the "unity of opposites", he does not so much see the world from the self, he sees the self from the view point of the world which forms itself. But still — and this is essential —action remains the centre of subjective-objective reality; action of the ego, the self, is identical with action of the world.

Logically, subject and object stand opposite each other, but reality is the "unification of subject and object, the self-unification of absolute opposites."[3] This self-united reality can be negated in one or the other direction, either the objective, or the subjective direction. According to Nishida the Western scientific mind in its noematic determination negates the real world of per-

---

1) "Die Einheit des Wahren, des Schönen und des Guten" p. 164.
2) "Die morgenländischen und abendländischen Kulturformen..."
3) ibid.

sonality, while the Indian and Taoistic philosophies in their noetic direction negate objective reality. The scientist regards reality as matter, the Buddhist regards reality as soul. "The Oriental religion of nothingness teaches: it is the soul which is Buddha". [1] Japanese culture is a culture of emotion where there is no difference between inward and outward: "hence the sensitivity of the Japanese towards things."[2]

As mentioned above, the perceived object transcends us and is still our sensation; in a similar way, we are submerged in the world and regain ourselves from the world. Emotion is identity in the contradiction of subject and object; we find ourselves in the world and the world finds itself in us. We can apprehend the world starting out from the ego, and apprehend the ego starting out from the world. In his treatise "Unity of Opposites" Nishida follows the second possibility. He no longer (as in the "Intelligible World") apprehends the "general" starting out from the ego; he understands the ego as an element of the Absolute. This Absolute, the last enveloping "nothingness", is not outside our world. Of course it is not in the world, either. It is in the oneness of transcendence and immanence,— it is but the unity of absolute opposites. The Absolute is not determined by something else, it determines itself. The result of this self-determination is the subjective-objective world. This world is therefore not determined by something

---

1) "Unity of Opposites" Chapter IV.
2) see page 50, footnote 1).

outside this world; the world is "self-determination with-out determiner." "Nothingness", like Hegel's "true infinite" (das gute Unendliche), can be grasped only in and by the finite. "The real", says Nishida,[1] "is the limited, the determined, the finite. The infinite has no reality. But the mere finite, too, is not the true reality. True reality must be the identity of finite and infinite."

For Nishida the real is also the true, "even the idea has birth and death."[2] Idea, according to Nishida, is that the world gives form to itself and sees itself as form; it is the form-character of the world. Idea and reality are not like two coordinated or subordinated worlds, an intelligible world and a real, sensual world. In the treatise "The Intelligible World", the world of ideas is reached by transcending, but this transcending goes only deep into the self. Even in that early period of Nishida's thinking the idea was at once transcendent and immanent. This contradiction is later brought to an extreme point. According to an old Zen saying "the true is the place where I am standing." There is no transcendent world of truth, and no metaphysical substance. The same is true for Nishida. There is but the one movement of self-forming of the formless, self-determination of "nothingness".

In "The Intelligible World" the road of philosophy leads from judgement to consciousness; in the depth of consciousness the idea represents self-contemplation of

---

1) In the treatise "Logic and Life".
2) "Unity of opposites" Chapter IV.

the pure "intelligible self". In the very core of this intelligible self, "nothingness" reveals itself as the "last enveloping". At that time the logical structure of being was determined as "being within" with reference to its "place", the specific sphere of categories. Now it is shown as concrete dynamic movement of reality. What was first called the "universal of absolute nothingness", is now called the "dialectical universal", but less with regard to its enveloping and determining function, than as the concrete whole. In Nishida's treatise "Unity of Opposites," his thinking follows the movement of the whole "dialectical universal" which encompasses nature as well as history. In this whole the physical world has its truth as one aspect of the historical world, seen from a point of view inside this historical world.

While Nishida in his earlier period departed from judgement and action, and by repeated transcending reached the deepest self as a pure mirror of nothingness, he now departs from this point which, however, is taken dynamically and is still action. The dynamic movement of the world is still a mirror for nothingness and a reflection of nothingness, but, as nature and history, it is acting reflection or "action-intuition". Self-determination of reality is, in itself, such acting reflection and is comprehended through acting reflection. Knowledge is gained in active intercourse with the world and is therefore "acting reflection" and historical. Intuition is, according to Nishida, "action-intuition" and not passive acceptance of an image of the world. It is a historical struggle of man and world, which is equivalent to a struggle of the world with itself.

The world of reality is essentially efficacy, productivity, creation — always in the sense of "action-intuition". There is no other effective, productive, and creative subject; therefore world is at once production and product, creation and created. Knowledge itself as a product of history is such production and product, it is itself a form of production of the world. Only through practice are we a mirror of reality.[1] Experiments and technology are such an acting reflecting intercourse with the world. In this sense the exact sciences are the best examples of "action-intuition". All knowledge is historical and gained by action-intuition.

If we want to understand the paradox of absolute nothingness being the world of reality, we must remember what has been said above about Mahayana Buddhism. In the Buddhist concept, world is Samsara as well as Nirvana, phenomenon as well as essence. The "dialectical universal" can not be conceived as a thing, as a substance or a multitude of substances. "In the core of the world there is neither one nor many."[2] The world as a whole is one, as much as it is many in its parts; it is identity in the contradiction of one and many.

Nishida considers real "that which, contradicting itself, is yet identical with itself." Therefore, to find reality means to seek contradictions. Nishida's dialectic is not so much the process of thesis, antithesis, and syn-

---

1) "Unity of Opposites" Chapter IV.
2) ibid., Chapter I.

6. PHILOSOPHY OF HISTORY

thesis, but a discovery of contradictions and the unity or identity in these contradictions. (This may perhaps be compared with Goethe's concept of "Polarität"). In Nishida's treatise "Unity of Opposites", much space is taken up in showing contradictions. In proportion to the stress placed on the paradox in Zen, Nishida has a tendency to heap up and repeat paradoxical phrasings of such contradictions.

The mirroring of nothingness in itself, understood merely as intuition (not "action-intuition"), would be an endless motion, infinite possibility of reflection and illusions, eternal play of free imagination. Since, however, the movement of the "dialectical universal" is "action-intuition", action must result. Action forms and decides. In so far as form and product have been decided, the product already belongs to the past. The fact, however, that such a product belonging to the past acts in the present and influences future decisions, makes us realize the "eternal presence" of the past. Nishida conceives the historical world as one single presence, in which the decided and formed constantly confront the deciding and forming. In this eternal presence, past and future meet. The dialectics of time, at which Nishida hinted in "Goethe's Metaphysical Background", is now explicitly analysed and reasoned out.

Time, the dialectical unity in the contradiction of past and future, has been called by Nishida "rotation in the eternal Now" or, in conformity with Leibniz, characterized as the present which carries the past on its back and is pregnant with the future. A third characterization, which is somewhat more difficult to understand, is that of historical time as eternal presence. Once Nishida, in a lecture, exemplified this by stating that the treaty of Versailles caused the second world war and was at the same time annulled by it. The past is present in a specific form, and the decision of the present, in turn, acts upon this form. In this connection the reader is reminded of what was said above about Shinto. Hardly any other country knows such an "eternal presence" of the past. In Japanese history the oldest past is still present, side by side with the newest forms of modern civilization.

The historical world moves from form to form and from present to present. Historical time runs in a straight line like physical time, and at the same time in a circle like time in the organismic world (from seed to seed). Historical efficacy is no longer causal action as in a mechanism, nor teleological action as in an organism, but a new and specific form of historical efficacy. The nature of this historical action is an "expression". The past, as a sepcific form, has its physiognomy and expression; it looks at us, it speaks to us, it threatens us, it tries to bring us under its spell. We, on the other hand, understand this expression and assert and defend ourselves in acts of expression. We make the world our expression. It is a struggle of life and death which takes place in our consciousness, which is at the same time the consciousness of the world. The world around us tries to make us a mere part of itself, while we try to make the world express us. We, as subjects, are submerged in our environment and have there our historical bodies. The surrounding world does not speak from the outside, but in ourselves with the voice of Satan; it has the mask of truth and speaks with abstract logic. Its truth is the logic of the produced and decided, of that which has been and has passed. It is our own deed which turns against us: "because it was this way in the past, you have to behave in this way now."[1] In opposition to this we ourselves represent the standpoint of future and free decision.

The consciousness in which past and future have found a synthesis can intellectually consider the world as given; but as concrete individuals of the historical world we are more than such an intellectual abstract as "consciousness in general". To us the world is given as a task. Here we must decide, here we have our being as selves, acting and reflecting ("action-intuition"). In being confronted by our own life and our own death, we are at the same time confronted, in our being as selves, by the whole of the world, by the Absolute. The result of such confrontation is, through action-intuition, a common "style of production". This is the common "style of production" of the "historical species", i.e. of the people. In the common cultural formation of a people the contradiction of the individual standing alone against the Absolute, has been overcome. The "historical species", the people, is the mediator between the many and the one.

---

1) "Unity of Opposites" Chapter III.

If, however, the individual acts only as a part of the species and conventionally, and allows himself to be determined only by the decided form of the past, then this would mean a relapse into causal action of the mechanism and would eventually lead to the death of the historical species. The creative productivity of a people lives only in and by its individuals. When the individual becomes uncreative the species comes to a standstill; and when the individual is creative, then that which stands behind him also becomes apparent in his work.

The historical movement of the world of reality is self-determination, which is at the same time self-forming and self-reflecting. It is the historical subject (historical species, people) through which the historical world forms itself by "action-intuition". But at the same time the world still remains a biological subject (biological species). And since the world forms itself, it is not merely forming as subject of history, but at the same time, formed, having the character of an environment. The world is at the same time forming subject and formed environment, it is a "unity of opposites". The world has in itself the contradiction of being subject and environment at once. This contradiction becomes conscious in man. The fact that man is torn, full of contradictions, may be called man's "original sin", and means the primary contradiction that man, as a part of the world, stands against the world, and that the world, which is the whole, stands against man in the form of environment.

The self-forming world transcends every form, and is yet immanent in each form, completely and essentially. In moving from form to form the world constantly renews itself. This renewal is not repetition of the same form, as it is in the world of physics; but true creation which transcends each newly gained form, and ascends from the merely formed and created towards the increasingly forming and creating. Nature is unity of opposites, i.e. of forming and formed, but the forming, the subject, the biological species, is still completely determined by the formed, the environment (adaptation).

Only in the case of man is there true self-determination, which includes consciousness and mind. Already in primitive societies we find crime and punishment, guilt and penance, which imply personality and mind. As in Hegel, the state is the perfect intellectual form of society and the moral substance of the historical species.

The process of self-forming of the world is at the same time self-representation (in nature and history), in which the individuals, as monads, mirror the world through self-expression (Leibniz). Basically the characteristics of nature are the same as those of the historical-social world, but not in the true, full sense. Nature is not yet a "true" unity of opposites. The individual does not truly express itself, it does not stand against the Absolute as "true" self-being. But history, as intellectual self-forming of the world, is the true unity of the opposites of forming and formed, the historical subject and the environment. They collide in the consciousness of man. The "categorical imperative" postulates that everybody ought to be also self-purpose (Kant). This means, according to Nishida, self-assertion of the individual in his nation, as a historical and creative personality against his environment. But the personality must keep in mind that it exists only in the whole of the people and in the whole of the world. When this is overlooked the result is moral self-overestimation. When it is kept in mind the result is self-dedication to the whole, or Faith. Religious faith as unconditional self-dedication to the Absolute, is in one respect unworldly, but in another respect it is in no way contradictory to the moral purpose of the nation. Religion differs from morality and is yet fundamentally one and the same. This becomes clear in the words of Shinran: "Even the good one will be saved" (how much more the evil one).[1] Religion is unworldly in so far as the individual faces the Absolute. But as unconditional dedication to the whole, religion affirms reality and is therefore not contrary to the moral purposes of the nation.

Already in his treatise "The Intelligible World," Nishida shows how being is revealed by self-negation in "nothingness". "Absolute negation is absolute affirmation."[2] In Zen unconditional acceptance of reality plays an important role; the Ego is illusion and does not stand against the world, it has "died" absolutely. In Nishida's

---

1) "Unity of Opposites" Chapter IV.
2) "Die morgenländischen und abendländischen Kulturformen".

philosophy of history and religion, the deepest "action-intuition" consists in having one's self in the absolute unity of the world of contradictions. That must be the reason why Nishida is so strongly attracted by Hegel's Theodicy, according to which "the real is the reasonable" (das Wirkliche ist vernünftig).

As has been mentioned above, knowledge of historical reality is not copying (Abbildung) of experienced reality as sensual being, but is itself a real historical process. In this process, man, himself a forming factor of this self-forming historical world, acting and reflecting in contact with the world (Goethe would say "im praktischen Gebrauch des Lebens"), gets in his grip the style of productivity of the world. Goethe says the best education is where the children grow up in their parents' world of labour; the Zen-Buddhist wants to get in his grip full life and inner freedom; in Japanese handicraft, mastering of the art is gained by practice (not through theoretical learning); in a similar way knowledge, according to Nishida, is self-forming of the world through "action-intuition". Here, technology and experiments have their significance and logical justification. Experience means experience of the style of productivity of the world. Knowledge is grasping the concrete concept (Hegel: "der konkrete Begriff"), and Nishida calls his theory of knowledge and his system of philosophy "concrete Logic". Like civilization in general, knowledge is historical self-formation. Man, by expressing himself in civilization, gives at the same time expression to the dynamic process of the world itself. Knowledge itself is history, is self-formation of the formless, self-determination of absolute Nothingness.

It is obvious that Nishida is dependent on Hegel in his concept of concrete logic and in his idea of ascending self-realization of the Absolute. But in conclusion the following differences can be pointed out:

1. Nishida's Absolute is not like Hegel's "Geist", personal and God in the Christian sense, but impersonal and nothingness in the Buddhist sense.
2. The historical individual is not, as in Hegel's philosophy, an absolute substance like the Christian immortal soul; it exists only through the medium of the historical species and is basically absolute nothingness.
3. World history is not, as in Hegel's philosophy, a progression through stages, moving from East to West, but an unfolding of various types of civilization, each being an immediate expression of the Absolute.
4. The "idea", which appears as an intellectual forming principle in the transition from nature to history, is not, as in Hegel's philosophy, the one idea, but an idea and a style of productivity which is continuously replaced by other styles of productivity.
5. The state, as moral substance, is the peak of intellectual achievement, but emotionally Nishida considers art and religion the true height of self-realization of the world, for here is the perfect

unity of opposites.

Nishida's treatise "Unity of Opposites" may be called a grandiose metaphysics of history as realization of the unreal, and at the same time a profound meditation on a Zen-problem: the form of the formless.

Directions for the Reader

Since the translator was very faithful to the original, the reading of the following essays is extremely difficult. The reader is reminded of all that has been said in the introduction about the peculiarities of Japanese thinking, and about the difficulties in following Nishida's thoughts.

Very many repetitions of formula-like phrases give the impression that there is no progress in thought. It is like climbing a mountain in serpentines. The climber has the impression that the view is the same at every curve. Only the careful reader will see the difference in the views, resulting from the increasingly higher standpoint.

The fact that Nishida uses many self-coined words, makes reading even more difficult. The reader, therefore, finds at the end of this book a small list of Nishida's favorite expressions with a short explanation.

Many references to occidental books give an impression of eclecticism, but Nishida's books were written for Japanese readers who find these references very helpful for the understanding of Nishida's philosophy. His "system" tries to give each thought its proper place.

An impatient reader is advised to read first the last chapter which is usually considered to be the most original and interesting one. But then the reader should start from the beginning again. The last paragraph, however, usually fades away like the finishing murmur of a Japanese poem or speech.

I. THE INTELLIGIBLE WORLD

by KITARO NISHIDA

1.

Knowledge, proceeding by judgements, may be called self-determination of the Universal[1]; in order that something be thought, the Universal must determine itself in itself. With regard to the Universal, three stages or layers can be discerned by which three worlds are defined. First, there is the Universal of judgement; everything that has its place[2] in this Universal, and is determined by it, belongs to the natural world in the widest sense of the word. Second, there is the Universal which envelops the Universal of judgement; it contains something that transcends the plane [or field] of predicates; it is the Universal of self-consciousness. Everything that has its place in this Universal, and is determined by it, belongs to the world of consciousness. Third, there is the Universal which envelops even the Universal of self-consciousness; it contains something that transcends the depth of our conscious Self. Everything that has its place in this last enveloping Universal, and is determined by it, belongs to the intelligible world.

This intelligible world transcends our thinking. Then, how can we think it? That something is being thought,

---

1) This concept is related to Hegel's concept of "das Allgemeine". According to Hegel, a judgement of knowledge has the form: "the individual is the universal" ("Das Besondere ist das Allgemeine").

2) Place ("basho") is the basic idea of Nishida's Logics, and is related to Plato's concept of "topos" as the "place of the ideas".

means, as was said above, self-determination of the Universal. If the intelligible world is thought through self-determination of the Universal, then: what kind of Universal is it? It seems to me that there is a way of comprehending the intelligible world by starting from our consciousness and its character of intentionality. An act of consciousness is, at the same time, real and intentional; it is noetic and noematic, at once. And that which is intended by an act of consciousness, is not only a content of consciousness, but has also trans-conscious objectivity. In cases when this can be understood as inner perception, the act of consciousness intends a past act of consciousness. But the act of consciousness can also intend something that transcends our consciousness; it can intend eternal truth which is thought as being in itself and being independent from whether it is actually thought or not thought. In the direction of such intended objects, i.e., in the direction of noema, the act of consciousness transcends our consciousness. But, at the same time, it transcends also in the direction of noesis, i.e., in the direction of action. That which is merely temporal reality in time, is not intentional; a psychological phenomenon can be intentional, but as long as it is merely temporal, it cannot intend trans-conscious objects. In order to intend something trans-conscious, our Self must transcend the conscious Self. Truth, for instance, can be thought only from the standpoint of Kant's "consciousness in general" ("Bewusstsein überhaupt"). In this case, the act of consciousness has no psychological reality, as belonging to one conscious Self; it has the mode of "being", like the transcendental Self, and belongs to this transcendental Self which is to be found within the concious Self.

If an intelligible world which transcends our world of consciousness is conceived, then the Universal which determines this intelligible world must transcend that Universal of self-consciousness which determines our world of consciousness. Its structure as enveloping Universal can be thought in analogy to the Universal of self-consciousness.

2.

What is the Universal of Self-consciousness? Self-consciousness is beyond the transcendental plane [or field] of predicates, and is essentially no longer determined by the Universal of judgement. Judgement is self-determination of that Universal. That which is determined by the Universal of judgement is essentially something thought, but not something thinking. It is content of judgement, but not making judgements. What is called Self or Ego, is beyond the determinations of space and time; it is the individual in the abyss of the individual in space and time. In thinking such an individual, it is implied that this individual has its place and is determined by a Universal. This can no longer be the Universal of judgement.

It must be a Universal which envelops the Universal of judgement. I have called it the Universal of self-

71

consciousness, because self-consciousness has its place in this Universal, and is determined by it. How is this new and enveloping Universal of self-consciousness determined?

If that which determines itself through judgements is called the "concrete" Universal, then this concrete Universal must have several planes of determination in itself, and in these planes it determines its own content. These different planes themselves are the "abstract" Universal. This abstract Universal is the unity of predicates, or the plane of predicates for each single being which can become a subject of judgements, but never a predicate. It is called abstract Universal, because it gives only one aspect of a single being which has its place in the concrete Universal. With regard to the Universal in general, the abstract Universal signifies the planes of determination, where the concrete Universal determines itself. The abstract Universal may also be called the plane of projection of the Universal itself, and it may be said that the abstract Universal reveals the meaning that the Universal contains the Universal. Corresponding to the transcendental plane of predicates — from the standpoint of the Universal of judgement —, there is the plane of determination — from the standpoint of the Universal of self-consciousness; it is the plane where the Universal of self-consciousness mirrors its own content. That which had its place in the transcendental plane of predicates, and was concrete and real, now becomes abstract and mere content of consciousness. That which is conscious of itself, the self-conscious, gets the meaning of "being in...", while all that had its place in the Universal of judgement (as its content), now becomes unreal, as content of the Universal of self-consciousness; the meaning of its "being" changes from that of an objective being to the subjective being of an act of consciousness.

, With regard to the form of the Universal of judgement, the self-conscious has the logical character of being only subject, and never predicate, while everything that has its place in the Universal of judgement, gets the meaning of a predicate. In this sense, the self-conscious is the pure theoretical self, by making the content of the Universal of judgement, such as it is, into a content of consciousness. The theoretical Self which has its place in the Universal of self-consciousness, is but empty and formal "being", which has not yet made itself the content of its self-consciousness. Therefore, nothing is added to the content of consciousness when it becomes such content of consciousness; only the meaning of Being as such is changed. I hope to clarify in what follows the peculiarity of consciousness and the essence of intentionality.

That which has its place in the Universal of self-consciousness, is at the same time objective and subjective; it has the character of an object in so far as it has its place also in the Universal of judgement, but it has, at the same time, the subjective character of a content of consciousness, because its very place is in the plane of consciousness of the theoretical Self. However, that which has its place in the plane of consciousness of the theoretical Self, as was said above, does not yet have its own self-conscious content. It does not yet, therefore, determine its own content;

it merely mirrors the content of something else which transcends itself; sensations of colour, for instance, (which, of course, are not the physical rays, but phenomena of consciousness) have, as such, a peculiar mode of Being namely that of self-consciousness. At the same time their content, which may be called "colour in itself", transcends self-consciousness. By coming nearer and nearer to the standpoint of the theoretical Self, this content becomes more and more transcendent, and the reality of consciousness of this content becomes more and more formal, so that there remains for consciousness only the meaning of "mirroring". This relationship is intentionality.

Since consciousness is regarded as active, one speaks of the activity of consciousness as of "acts". But this activity has no weight from the standpoint of pure theoretical knowledge, where the act-character is no longer a special content of reflection. The sensations of colours may be very subjective and individual, but their content is objective.

In order to make conscious the very essence of self-consciousness, as such, the meaning of "having its place in the Universal of self-consciousness" must be deepened, and the meaning of self-conscious Being, mirroring itself in itself, must become evident. In order to make this possible, a transition is required from the standpoint of the knowing Ego, or the theoretical Self, to the standpoint of the willing Ego, or the practical Self, which is the standpoint of an activity of activity. Then our consciousness realizes the full meaning of "self-consciousness mirroring its own content", while the meaning of the transcendental plane

74

of predicates of the Universal of judgement disappears.

Two definitions of the abstract Universal have been given which do not have the same meaning. The first definition said: The abstract Universal, contained in the Universal of judgement, is merely the Universal in general, containing no self-determination. The other definition said: The abstract Universal is merely the unity of the planes of predicates, or the unity of predicates. In the first definition, the abstract Universal has, though incompletely, the meaning of the Universal in general. In the second definition, it has already the meaning of a mediating plane for everything that has the character of "being in...". The more, therefore, the meaning is deepened so that the Universal determines itself in itself, the more does its abstract meaning in the first definition change into the mediating meaning in the second definition. In the same proportion a transition takes place in the Universal of self-consciousness, a transition from the plane of consciousness of the theoretical Ego to that of the practical Ego. The plane of consciousness, having its place in the Universal of self-consciousness, will still retain its character of intentionality. The content of consciousness, e.g. colours, can differ according to different noesis (remembering, reproduction, or imagination), but even when it becomes an object of will, it still retains a noematic character and still retains the property of something intended. Only, such content of consciousness is more then mere noema of an intentional act, more than something known from the theoretical standpoint. In order to reveal the essence of will, one must, starting from

75

intentionality, intend the activity of intending. Noesis must become noema, and the character of consciousness must become conscious. Instead of accepting two kinds of intentionality and consciousness, I follow the analogy of the Universal of judgement where the determined was the judgement, and I define all acts of consciousness as self-determination of "being", in the sense of being in the Universal of self-consciousness; so-called intentionality is its one abstract projection. Having its place in the Universal of self-consciousness, then, means knowledge. When this "being" [as being in] is merely formal, consciousness is theoretical, but true consciousness must have will-character. True intention is basically inner intention. Not intention, but will is the essence of consciousness. What is called intentionality, is but a weak willing. The general opinion that intentionality is the essence of consciousness stems from the fact that will is generally considered to have mere act-character.

Will is knowing efficacy and effective knowledge. Therefore it is essentially different from mere theoretical behaviour, from mere intention of an object. Efficacy is not knowledge; when we say "I am active", this "I" is known, but not knowing. The knowing "I" looks at the active "I"; it sees the change of the Ego. Seen from the point of view of intentionality in the knowing Ego, the intended is the intending, and vice versa. What, now, is the meaning of "I do", "I am active" for the knowing Ego? Doing means a change, means to become different. When the knowing-acting Ego changes the intention in the direction of the intending (i.e. towards the inward) it never reaches it; the intending envelops the intended, and between them there is a gap. On the other hand, if one separates both completely, there remains no identical Ego and, therefore, no such thing as "I do". In order to constitute an acting Ego, action must be notion or knowing, in each moment of its becoming different. Such knowing unifies the intending and the intended, and, at the same time, changes and becomes different itself. The acting Ego is a continuity of such a knowing Ego, and the acting Ego envelops the knowing Ego.

The knowing-acting Ego, i.e. the willing Ego, may be compared to a line; the single points of the line represent the knowing Ego, while the curve represents the content of the acting Ego. The knowing Ego, in which the intended is the intending itself, is already a point on the whole line; that means that the knowing Ego is already a willing Ego. A mere knowing Ego would be a straight line, a Zero curve. In this comparison, intention is the meaning of the direction of the points on the curve.

Seen from the act of intention, something noetic forms the basis of intention; a knowing Ego forms the basis of noesis, and the acting Ego, as was shown above, forms the basis of the knowing Ego.

Each concrete Universal has in itself planes of determination where it determines its own content. In the Universal of judgement, the abstract Universal corresponds to these planes of determination; in the Universal of self-consciousness, the theoretical plane of consciousness corresponds to them. There, the self-conscious determines itself: it is the reason why consciousness is intentional. It is in analogy to the Universal of judgement, where everything that is, has its place and is determined by predicates. That which has its place in the abstract Universal, is only determined by subsumption, without determining itself and without mediating itself with itself through this subsumption. In analogy to this, that which has its place in the theoretical plane of consciousness does not self-consciously determine itself, nor mediate itself with itself. The self-determinating and self-mediating act is not an act of intention, but an act of will. The process of the self-consciously determining its own content is will. Even the theoretical self-consciousness is self-consciousness only in such a sense. The act of intention, seen from the other side, is theoretical self-consciousness, which is the merely formal or empty will. Corresponding to the act of judgement, the self-determination of the Universal of self-consciousness is the act of will. And a willing Ego, having its place in the Universal of self-consciousness, corresponds to the single being which becomes the subject, but not the predicate of judgement. Seen from the point of view of the abstract Universal, the basis of judgement lies in the single being. If, however, judgement is taken as the self-determination of the Universal, the single being has its place in the transcendental plane of predicates; this single being, as determining itself, forms the basis of judgement. In the same sense, the subject of will, seen merely from the act of intention, is something transcendent. But if the act of consciousness (and also the act of intention) is taken as self-determination of the

Universal of self-consciousness, will, or practical self-consciousness, forms the basis of theoretical self-consciousness. Will forms the basis of self-consciousness, and self-consciousness forms the very basis of judgement. Judgement is an act of intention without self-consciousness; the act of intention is will without self-conscious content. It was said above that the abstract Universal was the unity of predicates for the single being, but it can now be said that the theoretical plane of consciousness is the plane of unification for the self-conscious will. This tendency becomes clearer as our self-conscious will deepens. In that the plane of self-determination of the Universal of self-consciousness becomes a plane of mediation for the willing Ego, or a common will, "social consciousness" is to be thought of as following this plane in the direction of noesis. At the same time, because the plane of self-determination of the Universal of self-consciousness still retains the function of a plane of predicates of the Universal of judgement in the direction of noema, the physical natural world in the narrow sense, that had been a world of objects of the theoretical plane of consciousness unified with the transcendental plane of predicates, now becomes the teleological natural world. This teleological world is determined in a transcendental plane of predicates which is, at the same time, the plane of self-determination of the will. So, the teleological world is not, like the physical world in the narrow sense, determined by the Universal of judgement in the strict sense.

79

3.

It has been said above that, starting from the act of intention, by transcending in the direction of noema and noesis, an "intelligible world" is to be thought which has its place in an intelligible Universal enveloping the Universal of self-consciousness. Our world of consciousness, which has its place in the Universal of self-consciousness, has become visible through the act of transcending in the direction of the predicates of judgement [in the direction of predication]. On the same basis, we now proceed further: consciousness must transcend even consciousness. What does this mean?

When a concrete Universal is enveloped by a more concrete Universal, there then appears a contradiction in the being which had its place in the first Universal, and so with the series of beings. For instance: that which has its place in the Universal of judgement, is mere predicate and becomes subject [due to the transition from Universal of judgement to the Universal of self-consciousness], and so contradicts itself [from the standpoint of the Universal of judgement]. This contradiction means action. While the self-determination of the Universal is intensified, the Universal gets less and less determinable from the earlier standpoint, and the determination is taken over by a "being in..." [in the enveloping Universal]; and what had been a mere "being in..." [the single being] comes to determine itself. So, the determination becomes contradictory [because the "determines" is the "determining"].

However, the content which has become indeterminable becomes positively determinable for the [higher] Universal which transcends and envelops the Universal of judgement; the content contains the contradiction in itself. That means: in the Universal of Self-consciousness an Ego, or Self, is determined [which contains and includes the contradiction.].

By analogy, the same is true for that which has its place in the Universal of self-consciousness. The Universal of self-consciousness determines that which knows itself; that which has its place here, has become contradictory in so far as knowing is, at the same time, being known, and the known is the knowing. The Self itself is the contradiction. The last and deepest "being", in the sense of self-consciousness, is the will. True self-consciousness is the will. True self-consciousness is not in the theoretical but in the practical self-consciousness. Only the acting Self has its content truly, and only willing is a true knowing of itself. It can be said that will is the height of self-consciousness, and that will is the last "being" which has its place in the Universal of self-consciousness. Will is, as many pessimists say, the point of contradiction: we desire in order to end the desire; we live in order to die.

In order that the conscious Self may transcend itself and enter a world of intelligible being, the Self must transcend its own will. In the uttermost depth of our will there is something which transcends and resolves even the contradiction of the will. This something has its place in the "intelligible world", and the transcending in the direction of noesis is, at the same time, a transcending in the direction of noema. While entering a transcendent world, there must be the possibility of consciousness of a transcendent object.

What does it mean to say that we transcend the will of our Self? That the Self is beyond the Self does not mean mere disappearance of the will; it does not mean mere disappearance of consciousness of the will. Will stems from consciousness of a purpose, and disappears when the purpose is fulfilled. In this sense will is a purpose-conscious act. That which is revealed at the end, must already be given in the beginning, in order to constitute such a purpose-conscious act. This act can, therefore, be called a process, which both contains the end in the beginning, and determines its own content. When that which, in such a manner, determines its own content is our Self, then this act of determination is an act of will. That which, in such a sense, is regarded as our true Self in the greatest depth of our will transcends and contains the will. Our will is founded on this Self.

When the Universal of judgement is enveloped and contained by the Universal of self-consciousness, and when the Universal itself no longer to be determined by the way of judgements, then that which had the last and the deepest place in the Universal of judgement reveals itself as action or as acting. The acting as "being" becomes full of contradictions [for the Universal of judgement]. It no longer has its place in the Universal of judgement. Something truly acting is not to be found in the so-called natural world. But when the Universal of judgement is enveloped by the Universal of self-consciousness, then an acting subject becomes visible behind action, and it can be said that the action is founded on something which acts. Something that truly acts, must have the character of consciousness.

In the process of determination within the realm of the Universal of judgement, subject and predicate stand against each other. Within the Universal of self-consciousness, they are lined as a kimono is lined with a precious silk [that overlaps somewhat and, somehow, envelops the kimono]. Now they stand against each other as acting and acted. In the same Universal of self-consciousness, this mutual opposition deepens and becomes the opposition of knowing subject and known object. Through self-consciousness, a mere act becomes first teleological, and then an act of will.

When the Universal of self-consciousness again is lined with an enveloping [Universal], then the last being which had its place in the Universal of self-consciousness, becomes the act of will which contains in itself the contradiction. Therefore, because it is contradictory in itself and can no longer be determined by the Universal of self-consciousness, the being which truly wills no longer has its place in the Universal of self-consciousness, and must have already transcended the so-called consciousness. It must contain in itself the opposition and contradiction of subject and object: it must see itself.

By analogy to that which has its place in the Universal of judgement, and determines itself through judgements, and by analogy to that which has its place in the Universal of self-consciousness, and determines itself self-conscious-ly, that which truly wills, determines itself by "intel-lectual intuition". This true willing may also be called creative productivity in so far as even knowledge means construction, and the opposition of subject and object means the opposition of constructive form and given material.

The true will may be called a weak intuition [as seeing itself], it is, so to say, an image of intuition, mirrored in our consciousness. When our Self transcends the will of the Self this transcending Self is no longer conscious, and it is beyond the limits of reflection. For our common sense and usual thinking, therefore, there is no such "be-ing" which could be called an "intelligible Self"; what we can think, is only the content of intuition or the content of that which is seeing itself. The — noetic — side, so to say, can not be seen; what is seen, is only the noematic side [the content].

The reason for this fact is that the "place" of a Universal which is enveloped by another Universal, and has its place there, forms the abstract plane of determina-tion for that [being] which has its place in the enveloping Universal.

I call "idea" ($\iota\delta\varepsilon\alpha$) that which could also be called the "noema" of that which is seeing itself. He who retains the standpoint of the conscious Self can think that which transcends this standpoint in no other way than as "idea". But this idea is always objective, and there is no subjective consciousness of this idea; not even the relationship between idea and subjective consciousness can be explained from this standpoint.

He who thinks a transcending Self does it already from the standpoint of this transcendental Self — if he really thinks something. Even when thinking a "natural world" as self-determination of the Universal of judgement, this Universal of judgement is already enclosed in the [intelligible] Universal which envelops the Universal of self-consciousness. That is because a judgement can be called "true" or "false" only then [i.e. from the standpoint of the intelligible Self]. Even the Self which has its "place" in the Universal of self-consciousness, can not yet be called normative; it is not the thinking Self itself, but the thought Self which has become an [psychological] object of thinking. Therefore, the intelligible world is not another world beyond and outside ourselves; we are within it ourselves.

Not only the natural world, but even the world of self-consciousness is still thought by reflection, and as such may be rightly called a transcendent object. That which is determined within the Universal of judgement belongs to the sphere of subjects of judgement, and that which is transcending in the depth of the plane of predicates is still thought by reflection, because of its negation as predicate, and its affirmation within the Universal of self-consciousness. In this sense, even the Universal of self-consciousness is still something determined, and not determining. That which has transcended it is now no longer to be determined through judgements. Only in so far as it makes a place for the Universal of self-consciousness (a plane of determination), where it

85

projects its own image, can it be said to be determined through judgements. One might call it self-determination of the indeterminable Universal. The true Self determines itself by mirroring its own image, and so we consciously see only the shadow of the Self.

The sphere of inner perception corresponds to the content of the individual self-consciousness, determined by the Universal of self-consciousness. In analogy to the Universal of judgement, where the individual being is that which becomes subject, but not predicate of judgement, or, in other words, that which encloses the predicates in its being as subject,—in the Universal of self-consciousness, the individual self-consciousness is that which intends itself directly. It is that which encloses the noema in the noesis. Everything that belongs to this individual self-consciousness, belongs to the sphere of inner perception. Something like social consciousness has already surpassed the sphere of inner perception.

4.

We go deeper and deeper into the noesis in the act of self-conscious transcending (transcending in the very depth of the will). At the same time a progressive enclosure of noema in the noesis takes place, while the meaning of "being" in the sphere of self-consciousness increases in significance.

In theoretical consciousness, the noesis does not yet enclose the noema, and the Self is not yet conscious of its own content. Where the noesis is the noema and where, therefore, the Self is conscious of its own content, the "feeling self-consciousness" is reached; the content of feeling reveals the mood and state of our Self. The feeling Ego is in the middle of the Universal of self-consciousness, just as the "thing" is in the middle of the Universal of judgement. The willing Self, however, becomes visible in analogy to "acting"; it becomes visible in the depth of the Universal of self-consciousness, which is already enveloped by the intelligible Universal. The willing Ego is, therefore, already beyond ordinary consciousness, and now it can be said that the noesis encloses the noema. But that which is beyond can no longer be called "being" in the sense of consciousness. That which is regarded as "being" in the sense of consciousness is merely "expression". What is expressed by this expression is the content of something that is beyond the willing Self.

In the relation of noesis and noema, the position of subject and predicate of judgement is already exchanged. That which had belonged to the sphere of predicates has become something real. When the noesis, by progressive enclosure of the noema, finally has even transcended the will, then that which had been regarded as transcendent object becomes the content of that which sees itself. The "being" is that which sees itself, and the object is submerged in the subject.

From the standpoint of the Logic of the subject, starting from the object [as subject of the judgement], the different changes in the noesis would appear as

87

changes of the object, and the self-transcendence of the Self would appear as submersion of the subject in the object. In such a Subject-Logic there would even be something like intellectual intuition, where subject and object are one and the same. In such a case the Self, limited to the conscious Self, would be mere subject of knowledge which has the truth as its object, but which should not be called "being" in any sense. If one thinks of subjectivity as contained in objectivity in such a way, it would be possible to call this objectivity, seen from the conscious Self, something infinitely creative.

On the contrary, I think of the Self as "being" which is determined in the Universal of self-consciousness. And with regard to a transcendent object, I think, on the contrary, of the Self as transcendent. Of course, this is a logical aspect, and the experience of the Self as such means, therefore, only that the Self sees its own ground [or basis], intuitively. On the other hand, it can be said that Logic is a kind of self-consciousness of the abstract self-consciousness. Anyway, philosophy necessarily takes the standpoint of Logic. If, therefore, a transcendent Self is thought at all, this must be justified logically. This justification must logically determine the content of knowledge, which is constituted by the transcendent Self. This is my purpose, when I think that the conscious Self, determined in the Universal of self-consciousness, transcends, and that this transcending is once more enveloped,— when I think of another Universal enclosing and enveloping the Universal of self-consciousness. In so far as this Universal determines something that sees itself, it may be called the Universal of intellectual intuition.

Speaking of intellectual intuition, one usually thinks only of subject-object unity, without freeing oneself from the traditional object-thinking. I mean by intellectual intuition just this, that the Self sees itself directly.

In the case of the Universal of judgement, the judgement is the act of determination; in the case of the Universal of self-consciousness, self-consciousness is this determination; in the case of the Universal of intellectual intuition or the intelligible Universal, determination is this very self-intuition or seeing itself.

In this intelligible Universal, enclosing something that sees itself intuitively, the first in the series of "beings" which have their place here, is something like Kant's "Bewusstsein überhaupt" (consciousness-in-general), or the "pure Ego", das "reine Ich". This transcends the depth of self-consciousness and sees its own conscious activity; it has transcended consciousness in the direction of noesis. That is why it can no longer be regarded as "being" in the manner of consciousness. But it still has the meaning of a self-conscious being, just because it transcends in the direction of the noesis. It is essentially the opposite of a noematic transcendent object, since it still has that meaning of a self-conscious being, or of the Self. All objective being has its foundation in this Self. In what sense can we say that such a consciousness-in-general [or pure Ego] " is " in the intelligible Universal? What is its position as "being in..." ?

Earlier it has been said that the theoretical Self was

the first in the series of beings, having its place in the Universal of self-consciousness, after having transcended the depth of the plane of predicates. But that which transcends even the last in that series of beings, namely the conscious will, and has its place as the first being in the intelligible Universal, is the "theoretical intelligible Self".

Each concrete Universal contains an abstract plane of determination where it projects itself. This is the function of the enveloped Universal. When the Universal of judgement, enveloped by the Universal of self-consciousness, gets this significance as a plane of determination, it becomes the plane of consciousness for theoretical self-consciousness. And analogously, when the Universal of self-consciousness, enveloped by the intelligible Universal, becomes the plane of determination of this intelligible Universal, it becomes the theoretical plane of consciousness for the intelligible Self. The theoretical Self, as was said before, does not yet have the content of the Self as such; it is mere formal or empty self-consciousness. In the same sense, the intelligible Self, the consciousness-in-general, which has been reached by transcending in the direction of the noesis, is also still formal. Having its place in the intelligible Universal, the very content of self-consciousness has the meaning or significance of "being". How is the content of the earlier Universal changed by the self-consciousness of the intelligible Self?

As long as our Self is not yet conscious of itself, it resembles the transcendental plane of predicates of the Universal of judgement; we see only the world of objects, determined by judgements. That world may also be called the natural world in the widest sense. When, however, our Self has become conscious of itself, it sees [the "world of consciousness"], determined in and by the Universal of self-consciousness. There are two worlds opposing each other: the natural world and the world of consciousness, as two sides of the same thing, only under different aspects. On the one side, the plane of consciousness still has the quality of the plane of predicates of the Universal of judgement; that which had been determined in and by the Universal of judgement can also be regarded as content of the conscious Self, mirrored in the plane of consciousness. On the other side, that which lies in the plane of consciousness may, at the same time, be regarded as determinable by judgements. But the conscious being, determined in and by the Universal of self-consciousness, is a "being" only when determined by the conscious Self.

Such mere content of self-consciousness, belonging to inner perception, directly determines itself through judgements, and only in this sense can it be said that that which has its place in the plane of predicates in the Universal of judgements is completely enveloped by the self-conscious, and: "the Universal of judgement has its object in itself". The direction of noesis, however, is not limited to self-consciousness, as has been said already, but surpasses even the depth of the will. In this sense, a transcending intention can be thought, mirroring the content of something that transcends consciousness. Seen from this point of view, all content of knowledge by judgement, of which it has first been said that it is

91

determined by the Universal of judgement, has now the meaning of something known and conscious, in the sense that the Universal of judgement has its place in the Universal of self-consciousness. Furthermore, it is not only determinable as such content, but, intended by a deeper noesis, it has also the meaning of being essentially determinable by the intelligible Universal. Here, indeed, lies the foundation of knowledge by judgements. Any content of consciousness, while it has become conscious, has also trans-conscious significance.

In the Universal of self-consciousness, noetic and noematic directions oppose each other. Even in the will, which is the last in the series of beings in the Universal of self-consciousness, these two directions can not unite positively. Will itself is contradiction and infinite motion.

When the Universal of self-consciousness has its place in the intelligible Universal, and is lined, deepened and enveloped by this Universal, all "being" which is in our self-consciousness, gets, by mirroring the intelligible world, a "normative" character, the character of values. Of course, one can not say that all "being" that is in our consciousness be immediately already normative, only because the Universal of self-consciousness has its place in the enveloping Universal. A world of pure meaning and value is thought of only in so far as the being which has its place in consciousness mirrors the content of something trans-conscious. Only in this sense, does the act of our consciousness intend pure meaning. If the root of noesis lies deep in the intelligible Universal and is determined by it, then the act of consciousness, mirroring the content of that which sees itself, becomes normative and becomes an act of realisation of value.

That which confronts and opposes our conscious Self as "objective world", transcends our conscious Self, and is nothing else but the content of Something, deep in our conscious Self; this "something" is the "intelligible Self". Of course, the content of the conscious Self, too, is nothing else but the content of a deeper Self, and this content is determined somehow; but in so far as this content is not determined by the conscious Self, it appears as "objective world" to the conscious Self. The title of "being" belongs only to the conscious Self, while that which confronts it is unreal and is a world of mere meaning, or — one step deeper — the world of truth. To this world of truth belongs everything that is determined in the Universal of judgement, besides belonging to the self-consciousness. When the Universal of judgement is thought of as being enveloped by the intelligible Universal, then all its content loses its significance as "being", and gets the significance of "meaning" or "value". When the Universal of self-consciousness is enveloped by the intelligible Universal, the conscious Self, too, enters into the objective world. Kant's "Bewusstsein überhaupt" (consciousness-in-general) is that intelligible Self, in this sense. Therefore, from this point of view, everything enters as object of knowledge into the world of values.

In so far as the Universal of judgement is enveloped by the Universal of self-consciousness, the theoretical self-consciousness is reached; when the Universal of self-consciousness is enveloped, again by the intelligible Universal, the conscious Self transcends itself and becomes the intelligible Self. This very thing is found in Kant's consciousness-in-general. The consciousness-in-general has already transcended our [psychological] consciousness, and is no longer, in any sense, "conscious being". The fact that our Self transcends in the direction of noesis also means that all content of our consciousness becomes content of that which sees itself, and that the Self, by submerging and denying itself, encloses and contains a world of objects. When this transcendent or transcendental Self is seen from the point of view of our ordinary Self, the concept of a subject of knowledge, which constructs the world of objects, is necessarily adopted. The plane of predicates, too, becomes necessarily constitutive when it becomes transcendent; it is no longer determinable by judgements, but is through and through a determining, i.e. by returning to itself, and determining itself by itself. When the plane of predicates has its place in the enveloping Universal of self-consciousness, its mode of determination becomes self-conscious determination; and finally, when it has its place also in the intelligible Universal, its mode of determination reaches the significance of categorial determination, which constitutes the world of objects of knowledge. Such categorial determination means that the subject of judgement submerges in the predicate, while the plane of predicates determines the "being" of the subject. In order that the last predicative may, as a constitutive category, constitute the object of knowledge, the Universal of judgement must once be enveloped by the Universal of self-consciousness, and then — by its transcending in the direction of noesis — have its place in the intelligible Universal. That is why in Kant's "transcendental deduction" the foundation is the "I think" (ich denke), which must be able to accompany all our perceptions and ideas.

The subject of knowledge has transcended the Universal of self-consciousness, enveloping the Universal of judgement; it has transcended it in the direction of noesis and gets its content of knowledge, because the Universal of judgement has its place in the Universal of self-consciousness. Knowledge without content could not be called objective, and would not be truth, which represents the content of the intelligible Self. Compared with the subject of knowledge which, by transcending theoretical self-consciousness, functions merely as plane of predicates, — compared with this subject of knowledge, the structure of self-consciousness functions as principle of the "given" ("Gegebenheit"). In Kantian philosophy self-consciousness is merely a theoretical one, and the principle of "the given" is merely formal self-consciousness. Kant considers the "given" to be something like the form of time. Our self-consciousness reveals itself in the form of time. The noesis is so formal that it merely mirrors itself in itself. It constitutes the form of time. By this formal noesis, the conscious noema becomes content of experience.

When the Universal of judgement unfolds itself, it becomes the "Universal of conclusion"; this means that such Universal of conclusion already has its place in the Universal of self-consciousness. Seen from the Universal

95

of judgement, its determination passes on to a "being within"; this "being within" determines itself, and its form is the form of time. It can be said that "time" is the form in which the particular determines itself universally. On the other hand, time can also be thought to be the action of self-determination when the undetermined Universal determines itself. Seen from the point of view of the Universal of self-consciousness, the formal noesis means that the Self becomes conscious in the Self. The form of such self-consciousness is, in my opinion, that which Kant calls "time" as "pure form of perception" ("reine Form der Anschauung"). But theoretical self-consciousness, as has been said above, is still formal. By making such formal self-consciousness the principle of the "given" ("Gegebenheit"), nothing else but the physical world would be "given".

It is possible, however, to conceive a teleological world of purpose, from the standpoint of the intelligible Universal. The meaning of the Universal of judgement, having its place in the Universal of self-consciousness, is deepened. This Universal of judgement has found its place in a self-consciousness of will-character, which is conscious of its own content. Here, the Self sees a teleological world. The subject of this seeing has already transcended the self-conscious will, and has entered the intelligible Self. But as merely theoretical Self, it has a formal being in the intelligible Universal, and can, therefore, be compared to Kant's consciousness-in-general. But it can think of the world of purposes as object of knowledge.

The standpoint of Kant's philosophy in its essence can, in my opinion, be thought of in the above manner. Now, how is the standpoint of modern phenomenology to be regarded in this connection?

Giving up any objective knowledge, and reaching the phenomenological aspect ("phänomenologische Einstellung"), also means achieving the standpoint of the theoretical intelligible Self which has surpassed the conscious will and sees itself. The phenomenological standpoint means the deepening of noesis; from here, the "essence" ("das Wesen") is "seen" ("angeschaut"). This "essence" is the noema of an intellectual intuition, by which the intelligible Self sees its own content.

In this respect it can be said that this standpoint coincides with that of Kant, with the exception that the self-consciousness, which is the principle of the "given" ("Gegebenheit") in Kant's philosophy, has been deepened, and thus has become the intelligible Self. Kantian philosophy emphasizes the constitutive function of the intelligible Self, which is the transcendental subject of the Universal of judgement; this theory does not deepen the idea that the transcendental subject in the Universal of self-consciousness is the principle of the "given". Phenomenology, however, emphasizes just this standpoint of the "given", the standpoint of intuition. This theory forgets that the intelligible Self, as transcending noesis, has constitutive significance for the conscious Self, namely that it constitutes the object of knowledge.

It is not possible to intend a transcendent object in our consciousness, if the noesis does not transcend in the depth of our conscious Ego. However far one might deepen the standpoint of the conscious Ego, it is still impossible to intend a transcendent object from this standpoint. But the standpoint of a Self, where a world of objects is seen by transcending in the depth of noesis, is the standpoint of the constituting subject, beyond the conscious Ego. Transcending in the direction of noesis, is a transcending in the farthest depth of the Ego of the act, [or of the Ego as act]. As long as one does not elevate oneself above the act as a "being" in the form of consciousness one has not yet reached the standpoint of phenomenology. The standpoint of a pure Ego which sees noema and noesis opposing each other, is essentially the standpoint of noesis of noesis, and has as the act of the act, constitutive significance.

Husserl started from Brentano's position who saw the essence of consciousness in intentionality; that is why Husserl's phenomenology has not yet freed itself from this standpoint. His pure Ego ("reines Ich") is something which has deepened the standpoint of perception and idea ("Vorstellung"). But such a standpoint must make it impossible to become conscious of an object of thinking, not to speak of an object of will. One may say that such consciousness may result from a synthesis of acts, but such a synthesis already means constituting a higher ranking content of consciousness; this very activity of constituting, this constitutive act, is true consciousness.

In consciousness, the realizing of an act is a [kind of intuition a], "seeing", and in this manner we become conscious of something, when we are thinking. That which is thought, may be called an object of an intention, but this would mean a "seeing" where we have returned to the standpoint of perception. By heaping up acts of perception, no different act [of thinking] can result. And if one were to add a different act, it would mean a different consciousness if that act should be an act of consciousness. The act of perception is not the foundation, to which more and more different acts could be added; it is the significance of consciousness itself which changes. The consciousness of perception is not deepened, but what is called "intention" is deepened and means that the content of an act of consciousness of a lower rank mirrors the content of an act of consciousness of higher rank. Now, each act of consciousness must be related to the Ego. A noesis is "real" ("reell") itself, i.e. it is something conscious of itself.

Seen from the point of view of the concrete Self as such, "intention" means constituting the content of the Self in the Self. Thinking that an act of consciousness without self-consciousness is impossible, one must call this very activity of constituting the essence of consciousness. The so-called act of intention is but the abstract side, the constitutive element being ignored. The act of intention is merely the standpoint of the conscious Self, but from this standpoint, the noesis itself cannot become conscious.

5.

I have treated Kant's standpoint of the consciousness-in-general, and the standpoint of modern phenomenology

99

as the two sides of the intelligible Self, which sees itself.

Transcending the basis of the will, one reaches the standpoint of the intelligible Self; this standpoint of the Self, which has transcended the so-called conscious Self, is the subject of knowledge, confronting the conscious Ego. This subject of knowledge builds up the world of objects. At the same time, it must be regarded as "intuitive" Self, which denies and contains all standpoints, and sees what is within itself. But it is not a consciousness which has become conscious of itself in a passive manner; it has become conscious of itself in an active manner. Therefore, it is by no means mere intention, but has essentially the meaning that the Self determines the Self; it is not merely intending something, but is also conscious of itself. That which sees, does not merely describe, but has in itself an object, it determines in itself the Self. By making itself immediately and directly its object, the meanings of different acts are determined.

It goes without saying that the intelligible Self in this sense can neither be determined as objective "being" within the Universal of judgement, nor as psychological "being" within the Universal of self-consciousness. It can no longer be determined at all as "being", like an object of knowledge. On the contrary, it itself determines all knowledge.

When, however, the concept of an intelligible Universal can be thought, and can be thought by an intention which transcends consciousness, then, and only then, the intelligible Self can be called "being", as being within this intelligible Universal and determined by it.

But that which is conscious in the Universal of self-consciousness, as psychological phenomenon, is nothing but the abstract content of such a transcendent and, at the same time, transcendental Self.

The transcendent Self mirrors the Self in its depth, by seeing itself [intuitively]. But even the intelligible Self cannot be regarded as true "being", because, as formal "being" in the intelligible world, [as theoretical Self] it does not yet possess the content of the intelligible Self as its own content. The content of the Universal of self-consciousness has changed its significance only formally. Therefore, this intelligible Self, though transcendent, is mere subject of knowledge; its content has lost the significance as "being", and is "value".

When the plane of consciousness is lined, deepened, and enveloped by this intelligible Self, everything that has had its place in the plane of consciousness, gets the mode or character of "meaning" and "value". That which is on the side of noesis, is seen as the formal Self, while that which is in the direction of noema, is seen as "value", as transcendent object. Kant's theory of knowledge remains on this standpoint. By starting from letting the knowing and the known oppose each other, and by defining knowledge as an act, it will be impossible to go further. But by starting from the transcending intention, as has been said several times, the determination of an intelligible Universal may become visible from this standpoint, and I believe that, by doing so, I may clarify the connection between metaphysics and logic better than was hitherto possible.

If our Self is regarded merely as the unifying point of the acts of consciousness, and if consciousness is regarded as realisation of acts, its transcending would mean nothing but a transcending in the direction of the object. When, however, the conscious Self is understood as "being", which is determined in the direction of the subject by the Universal of self-consciousness, enveloping the Universal of judgement, it is possible to think of a transcendent Self as a "being" which is determined in the direction of noesis by, a Universal, enveloping the Universal of self-consciousness. When the Universal of judgement was enveloped by the Universal of self-consciousness, the plane of predicates of the first Universal became in the second Universal the plane of consciousness for the theoretical self-consciousness; and that which has its place here, intends as noesis the noematic object. Now, when the Universal of self-consciousness is enveloped by a third, the intelligible Universal, the plane of consciousness of the universal of self-consciousness becomes universal, in analogy to the former, the plane of consciousness for the transcendent Self; that which has its place here, intends a noematic-transcendent object; at the same time, there must be also a transcending in the direction of noesis.

The true "being" in the Universal of self-consciousness must be will, because the theoretical noesis, as conscious "being", is incomplete. The true Self is not in the theoretical, but in the practical self-consciousness. The will intends in itself, and the intention of the will is at once a mirroring of the Self in the Self. Seen in this way, there is the will behind the theoretical intention. That which is seen as noema is the mirrored content of the will.

The normative consciousness, in the plane of consciousness of the transcendent intelligible Self, could also be called "intelligible noesis"; it is an incomplete intelligible Self, and its transcendent object is merely a mirrored image, merely a seeing of the content of the intelligible Self. Taking this intelligible noesis merely as subject of knowledge, the noema loses its significance as "being", and becomes "value". Thinking of the noesis as completely disappearing in the noema, the noesis becomes a metaphysical reality like Plato's idea. In metaphysical reality, the noesis is completely submerged in the noema. Thinking of the noesis as contained in the noema, in the phenomenon of consciousness, the perception is regarded as conscious being in the sense of a psychology of perception; if, now, in the transcendent plane of consciousness an analogical procedure takes place, it is the phenomenological method, since the standpoint of phenomenology, as has been said above, can be regarded as a deepening of the aspect of perception in the "consciousness-in-general". From this standpoint, the Platonic "idea" loses its metaphysical reality, and becomes the phenomenological "essence" ("Wesen").

In order that each Universal may determine itself, there must be different acts of determination, by which the different Universals are distinguished from each other, and related to each other. In the case of the Universal of judgement, this act of determination is the act of judgement, and in the case of the Universal of self-consciousness it is the act of consciousness. The relationship between subject and predicate of judgement becomes that between noesis and noema in the Universal of self-consciousness. The more the Universal returns to itself, and the more the "place" approaches "Nothingness", the more the act of determination is taken over by a "being-within", and the being-within becomes gradually something that determines itself. In the case of the Universal of judgement, the being-within is the single being which encloses the being of the predicates; it becomes a mutual determination of single beings through predicates, and, finally, it becomes efficacy or "acting". In the Universal of self-consciousness, noesis and noema oppose each other; the more the Universal of self-consciousness returns to itself, in other words, the more it finds its place in a greater enveloping Universal, transcending itself, the more is the noema enclosed in the noesis. In the theoretical self-consciousness, noesis is but formal "being", but in the practical self-consciousness, the noema is enclosed by and in the noesis; the transcending in the depth of the conscious Self, therefore, means, as has been said above, a transcending in the depth of the noesis which has will-character. A transcending of the will itself, which is the root of the Self, may be impossible, but still we are conscious of the will. Are we not thinking our own will? Will becomes conscious, when the Self intends in the Self, and the intending is somehow the intended; will is conscious, in so far as the noesis has become noema, and vice versa. Compared with the noema, the noesis is always transcendent, and compared with the theoretical

104

self-consciousness, even the content of will is outward, is transcendent. Still, theoretical and practical self-consciousness are not two different things. The Self, having will-character, is conscious when theoretical self-consciousness is the abstract determination of practical self-consciousness, and when the content of the will is determined and noematically mirrored in the form of theoretical self-consciousness.

But, when the "being" in the direction of noesis no longer noematically mirrors the content of the Self, in other words, when the noema has surpassed and is beyond the conscious noesis, then our Self has already transcended the depth of the will. This can be thought of as being the "acting Self". An acting Self, in this sense, is in the depth of our conscious Self. Our conscious Self has been determined from the standpoint of such an [acting] Self. The content of this acting Self can be regarded as outward or transcendent by the conscious Self; but that content is more than this, it is the content of a deeper Self. It is that noematic content which becomes visible by transcending the Self in the direction of noesis. Here lies the root of the transcending intention.

The content of will is originally not theoretical noema; but the Self which has will-character is still determined by self-consciousness, as the last which has its place in the Universal of self-consciousness. The Self which has will-character, may be regarded as mirroring itself on the plane of consciousness. It can be said that it has not yet given up the congruence of noesis and noema, i.e. it has not left the unity of so-called inner perception.

It is similar to the content of the single being which does not belong to the abstract Universal. In spite of this, the single being, functioning as subject but not as predicate, is determined by and in the Universal of judgement, and furthermore is thought of as "acting". When the conscious Self is reached by transcending the depth of the plane of predicates, this [Self] — as the last "being" which had its place in the Universal of judgement, — is no longer determinable [by judgements]. But its noema can at least be thought of as content of the Universal of judgement. In a similar manner, the "acting Self" becomes visible by transcending the Self which has will-character; it is, even as the last being in the Universal of self-consciousness, no longer determinable [in the way of self-consciousness or psychologically], but its noema can at least, be thought of as content of the Universal of self-consciousness.

"Acting" means taking into the Self the outward world, which transcends consciousness. "Acting" means that I make a happening in the outward world an "expression" of my Self, as realisation of my own will. In this case, objective reality does not become an immanent "being" [in the Self, or] of the Self; it remains objective reality. And the subjective Self does not leave the Self; it does not become an objective Self. On the contrary, by our actions we become, in a deeper sense, conscious of ourselves. Such a Self envelops and encloses the outward world, by transcending the consciousness of the Self. The Self, through such "objectivation", deepens itself.

Since the expression of the will is, at the same time,

a happening in the outward world, and can be looked at theoretically, and since the content of will is, at the same time, content of consciousness, the usual opinion is that will is only the union of these two sides, and is enclosed only by theoretical self-consciousness.

In order that a happening in the outward world can be thought of at all, a consciousness, consisting of perceptions, is first required; without supposing [acts of] intention of perception-like noesis, no outward world could be conceived. But no "action of will" can be thought, by supposing only such acts of intention. In order to think "action of will", the noesis must have, from the start, a different meaning of intention. Furthermore, the desiring will, which is connected with perception, and which has in itself something of transcendence in the direction of noesis, transcends the determination of theoretical self-consciousness.

By deepening the meaning of such noesis-transcendence, a "being" can be thought of which has its place in the intelligible Universal, a being beyond the "consciousness-in-general"; this consciousness-in-general has been thought of as noesis-transcendence of theoretical self-consciousness. In other words, one can think even the content of the intelligible Self.

At the transition from the Universal of judgement to the Universal of self-consciousness, it was possible to make evident the transcending of the plane of predicates, by the thought: "I am conscious of myself". Now, at the transition from the Universal of self-consciousness to a further enveloping "intelligible" Universal, one can make

107

evident the transcendence of noesis, by the thought: "I know that I am acting".

Here I would like to add a word about that which we call "my body". We usually think that without body there is no soul, and the soul is dwelling in the body. What is the "body" in that case? That of which we are conscious as our sensual object, is essentially something in consciousness, and not something that offers a dwelling to consciousness. Kant's Ego is the basis of consciousness, as has been shown above. The body is an expression of our acting Ego, and has the significance of belonging to the basis of consciousness. Seen from the standpoint of the conscious Self, the body could be regarded as an organ of our will. But the body is not a mere instrument, but an expression of the Self in the depth of our consciousness. In this sense, it can be said that our body has metaphysical significance. The content of our Self requires acting. Our true Self reveals itself, when soul and body are identical.

6.

Starting from the act of intention, and transcending it in the direction of noesis, a formal "being" in the intelligible Universal is reached. This is nothing but a "consciousness-in-general", and philosophy content with this is nothing but theory of knowledge.

If one agrees however, that it is possible to penetrate into the intelligible noesis by self-consciousness of the "acting Ego", one can clarify in what sense a "being in the intelligible world", can be called "being", and how its content is mirrored in our consciousness.

In the case of the Universal of self-consciousness, too, the theoretical self-consciousness, making the plane of predicates a plane of consciousness, is not something that makes conscious its own content, it is not the true "being" in self-consciousness. It is the practical self consciousness, or will, which makes itself its object, and is truly conscious of itself. It is "egoism", the love of oneself, which determines the existence of the Ego in the realm of consciousness. Then, by transcending in the direction of noesis, i.e. by penetrating into the depth of the Self, the Universal of intellectual intuition, or the intelligible Universal, is reached. Among the beings in the intelligible world, not the consciousness-in-general, but the "self-consciousness of the acting Self" is truly "being".

The acting Self makes the world of objects an instrument of its own self-realisation, it makes the world its expression. (In loving an object, it loves itself.)

From this standpoint, the "consciousness-in-general" could also be called "formal acting Self", just as the "theoretical self-consciousness", enclosing no noetic content, could also be called "formal self-consciousness of will" or formal practical self.

Just as the practical Self transcends the plane of consciousness of the theoretical Self, and mirrors its own image in it, so the acting Self, as thing-in-itself ("Ding an sich"), transcends the world of objects of the "consciousness-in-general", and mirrors its own image in it. So, the world of objects of knowledge, and the intelligible world are connected by self-consciousness of the acting Self.

In this sense, our acting, first, determines the "being" in the intelligible world. This does not mean that a "knowledge" of the intelligible world is also effected by this self-consciousness of the acting Self. That would already be metaphysics. What I want to do, is to clarify in what way a metaphysical Being can be thought of at all, and what is its significance in relation to our world of objects of knowledge.

The acting Self has been thought of as transcending the depth of will, and reaching that which has its place in the intelligible Universal (the Universal of intellectual intuition), and "acting" has been thought of as determination of the intelligible Universal; but this is true only for the border of transition from the second to the third Universal; it is not yet true self-determination of the intelligible Universal. The opposition of subject and object remains from the standpoint of the acting Self; transcendent noema and transcending noesis confront each other, when seen from [the standpoint of] consciousness. This opposition [of noesis and noema] which stems from consciousness, must disappear from the standpoint of the intelligible Universal. The noema must submerge in the noesis, and the world of objects must be "subjectivated" through and through. Not before the "artistic intuition" is reached, can we determine the true "being" in the intelligible Universal, i.e. that which determines its own content. Here, "acting" means "seeing". Or, as Plato says, acting is a detour of intuition.

That is the reason why I call the Universal determining the intelligible world, i.e. the intelligible Universal, also the "Universal of intellectual intuition". Of course, that which has its place in the furthest depth of the intelligible Universal, has left behind even artistic intuition. In the case of artistic intuition, the noema of consciousness is submerged in the noesis; but this does not mean that the noema itself is annihilated. The contraposition remains, and the intelligible noesis is bound to the noema.

At the [highest] point of transcendence, i.e. at the point of deepest reflection, there is [again] the analogy to the Universal of self-consciousness; there the last "being" was the will; so there must be something in the intelligible Universal that has the significance of transcending the intelligible noema, as the last "being" which has its place in the intelligible Universal, i.e. there must be something that only sees itself. This "something" is the moral Self in the widest sense, i.e. "conscience".

I think of "intellectual intuition" as of an act of determination of the Universal, enveloping the Universal of consciousness. In this way, I want to think of an "intelligible world", similar to that of Plato and Plotinos. But all the "being" is transcended only in the direction of noesis, and not in the direction of noema. Intellectual intuition is not union of Self and "idea", nor union of subject and object, but the Self seeing immediately itself or the Self seeing its furthest depth. The "idea", as content of such self-intuition is that which becomes visible in the direction of the transcendent noema.

111

The first "being" in the Universal of intellectual intuition (intelligible Universal), namely as formal intelligible Self, is something like the "consciousness-in-general". This, taken as merely that which transcends the conscious Self, loses significance as "being", and becomes pure consciousness of norms, confronted by values. But, taken as intelligible Self, in the above sense, then it is constitutive, as a kind of acting Self. As that which sees itself, it can also be thought of as that which sees the idea of truth. But, in so far as it represents within the intelligible Universal something like an "intellectual self-consciousness", and in so far as it has the significance of a "place" for the Universal of self-consciousness, it makes the content of that Universal its own content, and therefore does not have its own content. It only formally changes the content of the Universal of judgement, enveloped by the Universal of self-consciousness, with regard to its significance, not to its "being". Thereby, however, the content of the intelligible Self is not to be "known" as truth, since it belongs to the world of "things in themselves" ["Dinge an sich"].

The content of the intelligible Self is first visible, as such, in "artistic intuition". That which had its place in the Universal of self-consciousness, as true "being", had to intend itself, and the noema had to return to the noesis. In such a sense, the willing Self was the point and the last "being" in the Universal of self-consciousness. But that which had its place in that Universal of self-consciousness in the most harmonious sense, by realizing the congruence of noema and noesis, was the "feeling

Self". Emotion can be called the content of our own conscious Self, in the most adequate sense. From the standpoint of the self-intending, the feeling Self is determined as quiet, static unity. Supposing that intention is a "mirroring", and that the noema mirrors the image of the noesis in the noesis, then the feeling Self is an image of the Self, mirrored in the Self. Egoism, or love of the Self is fixing this image as the Self. As in the Universal of self-consciousness, a concrete being becomes in such a way conscious of its own content, so, in the intelligible Universal, something can be thought of which sees itself and realizes the congruence of intelligible noema and intelligible noesis: it is the Self of artistic intuition, i.e. it is that which sees the "idea" of beauty. Therefore, artistic intuition is realized by forgetting the mere conscious Self, by loving the thing itself, directly as one's own Self, and by identifying oneself with it; then, artistic intuition reveals itself as content of our feeling.

The content of beauty does not at all enter the horizon of knowledge, because that which sees itself in artistic intuition, has transcended the abstract standpoint of the consciousness-in-general, and directly sees the content of the intelligible Self. Beauty is the form of appearance of the idea itself; it is only in artistic intuition that we have an intuition of the idea; only the beautiful is a visible representation of eternity on earth.

The "idea" can no longer be seen intuitively, in further progressive transcending in the direction of noesis. The noesis loses noematic determination, and becomes the Self of the "practical reason" ["praktische

Vernunft"], in the widest sense. It is similar to the Universal of self-consciousness, where the last "being" which had its place there, namely the will, was no longer noematically determinable, and the noema was, without mediation, the noesis. In the Self of practical reason, the noema is completely submerged in the noesis, and the intelligible noesis is conscious as "conscience" in the very depth of consciousness. Conscience has left behind all artistic intuition, and the soul sees itself in its greatest depth without mediation in the form of the acting Self. According to the Kantian School, the Self may be called the subject of the Ought [Subjekt des Sollens]. The moral Self is the true normative subject, but the subject-in-general may be called the normative subject of the Ought, though only in a formal sense. [Truth here being regarded as worth or value]. Compared with the normative subject as intelligible noesis, the noema is the "norm" or the "value". Since the consciousness-in-general possesses no content of self-intuition, and because the content of the moral Self is infinitely deep, both see only the "thou shalt!" in the direction of noema. The idea of the good cannot be seen [intuitively]. There is only moral development and infinite progressing. Only in the direction of noema is there something visible like an "intelligible character". But the intelligible character is not "seen" like the idea of beauty, but is merely an ideal.

In this way, I want to think of the "intelligible world", and discuss the differences and relationships of the "beings" which have their places in this intelligible world. But this does not mean that the intelligible world

114

would become an object of our knowledge! No, here I am consistently retaining Kant's standpoint. However, I am convinced that Kant's subject of knowledge can be thought of as the intelligible Self, by having a fundamentally different understanding of "knowing". As long as one adheres to the standpoint of the subject of knowledge, the intelligible world, as a world of things in themselves, is totally unknowable or unthinkable and transcendent. Since Kant recognized as principle of given material only a consciousness of perception, only something like the "natural world" was to be thought of as a world of objects of knowledge. However, by deepening the significance of self-consciousness, as principle of the "given", one reaches from the natural world the world of purpose (one reaches from the natural physical world the natural teleological world), and then the psychological world, which has self-consciousness as its object, and finally the historical world. All this belongs to the very world of objects of knowledge, and not to that world in which our true Self, the intelligible Self, has its place. Our true Self is not the Self that lives and dies in the historical world. That which lives and dies in the historical world is the so-called conscious Self, a shadow of the intelligible Self. Our true Self dwells in the intelligible world, which is conceived by deepening the meaning of self-consciousness in the depth of consciousness-in-general. In this sense, the deepest which is thought here is the moral world.

In the degree in which the concept of self-determination of the Universal is deepened, the determination is

115

passed over to a "being within", and the "being within" becomes self-determining. With this, the Universal becomes something that is no more determinable as Universal; it gets the significance of a "law" which confronts the "being within". It is that which, in the Universal of conclusion, was the Universal of the terminus major, confronting the Universal of the terminus minor. Something of the character of the terminus major, connected with something of the character of the terminus minor by "time" as terminus medius, forms a single Universal, and this is the natural world. Since in the Universal of self-consciousness that which has subject-character has already transcended the depth of the plane of predicates, it can not be said here that that which has the character of terminus major encloses the subject through "time". There is no "law" in the strict sense in the field of phenomena of consciousness. Taking "intention" as a quality of consciousness, and taking "intending" as mirroring, where that which has transcended the depth of the Universal of judgement mirrors its image in the plane of predicates, no phenomenon of consciousness can be thought to be independent of time. But the time of phenomena of consciousness is different from the time of phenomena of the natural world, since past and future cannot be united under a terminus major. The time of phenomena of consciousness has merely the tendency to unite something of the character of the terminus minor with something of the character of the terminus major. Historical time, too, is but a border case of such time; history has nothing of the character

116

of the terminus major.

That, however, which transcends even the Universal of self-consciousness, and has its place in the intelligible Universal, has transcended time altogether. Its "existence" is not determined by time, although that which exists in time is its image. That is why it can be said that the content of the "consciousness-in-general" is or exists in itself, independent of whether someone actually thinks it, or not. But since this consciousness-in-general, as merely formal intelligible Self, does not possess its own content, its ideal content, namely the intelligible noema, is without mediation the content of reality. The real world can be regarded as a direct manifestation of the intelligible noema.

In the case of the artistic intuition, the real world can no longer be regarded as a direct manifestation of it [the intelligible noema], and this is the reason why beauty is regarded as beautiful illusion. In the artistic intuition, intelligible noema and intelligible noesis are in perfect harmony. The noema does not disappear in the noesis; therefore, the noema of the artistic intuition does not free itself from the real world, being the intelligible noema of the consciousness-in-general. The real becomes "expression".

Finally in the moral conscience which sees itself, the noema has completely left behind the plane of consciousness-in-general, which could be called the abstract plane of the intelligible Universal; it has not even the significance of being mirrored there. The idea of the good has not even the significance of being mirrored in the real world, nor can it be said that anything real be its expression.

When the determination of the Universal passes on to the "being within", only "laws" are seen in the direction of the Universal. So now, only something like "moral laws" are to be seen in the direction of noema. And that which is regarded as "moral reality", like family or state, is not, like a piece of art, image or expression of the idea. All "being" has here the significance of "shall be". As in the case of the last "being" in the Universal of judgement, namely the "acting", the subject became predicate, and the predicate subject, and as in the case of will, the intending became the intended, so now, all "being" has become a "shall be", and that which has the character of a "shall be" has become a being. Something like moral reality can be compared with an eternally unfinished piece of art.

When, in such a sense, noema and noesis have separated, and the content of the Self can no longer be seen as noema of an intellectual intuition, then in the direction of noesis the "free will" is visible A formal moral philosophy, like that of Kant, is here established. In the moral Self, form and content confront each other always. But the moral Self does not see an alien content, like the theoretical Self, as formal "being", the conscience sees itself. That which shows itself objectively as moral reality is nothing but the content of the Self. In this sense, as intelligible Self, it is the same as that of the artistic intuition, with the exception that it can not find adequate expression. Ethics without content is no true morality. There is no intelligible Self without noematic relation. When the conscience sees itself noetically, the noematic lawful "moral world" is established. But because its content itself can not be seen directly, and does not stand before us as intelligible noema, the moral Self is thought of as acting Self, from the standpoint of the conscious Self. While in noetic transcendence the moral will is conceived in the noematic transcendence it is the objective moral world. The good as form, and the good as content, confront each other. However, the moral world is "created" by the moral Self; the purpose of the moral action consists in itself, i.e. in the creation of its own world.

The relationship between intelligible and real world needs further consideration, but I must limit myself to what I have said.

7.

Above it has been shown how, starting from intentionality, and transcending the last "being" in the Universal of self-consciousness, namely our conscious will, I conceive the intelligible Universal and I think of "being within", in the direction of noesis as three layers of the intelligible Self: intellect, feeling, and will. These three steps of transcendence can be thought, because the intelligible Self has transcended the conscious Self.

Transcending the will means, first, that the Self transcends the thought Self, that the consciousness transcends the conscious consciousness; an intellectual intuition

119

is reached, where subject and object are united. The intelligible Self is conscious of itself in intellectual intuition; it sees itself directly. Until now, philosophy has thought of "transcendence" only in the noematic direction. Therefore, speaking of an intellectual intuition meant already the end. I am, however, of the opinion that in that which sees itself, those three layers can be distinguished by transcending in the direction of noesis. The content of the act of consciousness as transcendent object is the "idea": the three layers of the intelligible Self are that which sees the idea of truth, that which sees the idea of beauty, and that which sees the idea of the good. The mere theoretical intelligible Self, similar to the theoretical self-consciousness, is but formal; it does not truly see the content of the intelligible Self, and it does not see its own content without mediation. Truth is the abstract side of the idea. The content of the intelligible Self is first seen in the noesis of feeling; in the artistic intuition we see the idea itself. The willing noesis, finally, sees the Self itself; it is the conscience, and the idea is practical.

Having left the will behind us, we elevate ourselves to the standpoint of the intelligible Self, and regard it, from the standpoint of the conscious Self, as creative. Even the theoretical intelligible Self is constitutive, as "consciousness-in-general". Only it remains mere subject of knowledge, because it does not see its own content. In the artistic intuition, however, seeing is creating, and creating is seeing. (Here, the Self is creative in the true sense.) Finally, in the case of the intelligible will, where the idea can no longer be seen objectively, it is analogical to the conscious will, which is the last "being" having its place in the Universal of self-consciousness; the intended was the intending, and the content of will was no more determinable noematically. In analogy to that, in the intelligible Universal, the intelligible will is no more object of possible intellectual intuition. The idea being purely practical, the "free will" becomes evident in the direction of noesis, and the intelligible Self is thought of as "free personality". Seen in this way, everything that has its place in the intelligible Universal is "personal". The world of ideas being the world of objects for the acting Self, the idea of the good, the highest idea, has regulative significance.

The truly concrete idea is personal and individual. This is because the intelligible personality, which is the last "being" having its place in the intelligible Universal, is individual. The idea, too, as its content, must be individual. Here lies the origin of individuality. The idea of truth, as content of the consciousness-in-general — in analogy to that which was mirrored on the plane of consciousness of theoretical self-consciousness — must be the image of an individual idea, and at the same time still universal and abstract. However, the truly individual and personal idea, though idea, does not have the character of noema, in the sense of something seen.

Only in the case of the idea of beauty can we see an individual idea. Since the truly personal and individual idea can no more be seen noematically, the idea of the good, having law-character, is merely regulative,

similar to the terminus major in the Universal of conclusion.

In this way, I think, it is possible to determine everything that has its place in the intelligible Universal, and
to clarify its relations. Thus, the connection and the
justification of the various philosophical standpoints can
be determined and clarified.

Kant's philosophy, taking the standpoint of the theoretical intelligible Self, cannot go beyond the truth which
forms the content of the formal Self. That is the reason
why Kantianism remains theory of knowledge. It is true
that Kant, too, starting from conscience, conceived the
Intelligible, but he neither connected these two standpoints, nor did he give a principle of determination of
the content of the Intelligible, of the content of the
beautiful and the good. Husserl deepened the consciousness of perception as far as the intelligible noesis.
But from this phenomenological standpoint, only one
side can be seen, namely the theoretical intelligible Self.
Fichte, by deepening the significance of the theoretical
self-consciousness, reached the acting Self. Fichte, it can
be said, takes the standpoint of the practical intelligible
Self, while Schelling, starting from artistic intuition, takes
the standpoint of the feeling intelligible Self. Hegel,
I would like to say, widened the meaning of reason to the
determination of the intelligible Universal. His philosophy is all-embracing. But it must be said that his philosophy merely deepened the theoretical standpoint through
and through, and therefore never reached beyond the
noematic determination of the intelligible Universal.

Everything is based on noematic transcendence, and the principle of determination of the noesis was not made clear. Fichte and Schelling, too, thought of will and intuition merely as acts; the willing one and the seeing one do not enter their perspective. No individuality, no individual freedom of will, can be clarified later by such a way of thinking. (It can be found, though, in Schelling's late works, but without logical foundation.)

To enter the intelligible world, by transcending Kant's standpoint noematically, would already mean going beyond the standpoint of critical philosophy, and a trespassing into the field of metaphysics would be inevitable. Kant gave no principle of noetic determination, but he stuck to the standpoint of the formal intelligible Self. He did not go beyond it. Therein lies, I think, the peculiarity of his philosophy.

The intelligible can not be discussed at all, without clarifying the basis of noetic determination, and its relationship to our consciousness. There is the danger of onesidedness, by starting from one layer of the intelligible Self, and trying to clarify the others from there. The content of truth, beauty, and the good can be comprehended and clarified in their relationship only by looking back into the depth of the noesis.

I have thought of the Universal of self-consciousness as enveloping the Universal of judgement, and of the Universal of intellectual intuition, or intelligible Universal, as enveloping the Universal of self-consciousness. Seen from the intelligible Universal, the enveloped has its foundation in it [the enveloping]. In so far as intelligible

123

noesis and intelligible noema still confront each other in the intelligible Universal, and in so far as the intelligible noesis, i.e. our true Self, is still noematically determined, the conscious Self is determined [as the enveloped]. The Self is made an object, and so the Universal of self-consciousness is constituted. Seen from the standpoint of mere noematic determination, the noesis slowly disappears in the noema, and a kind of substratum is determined that can be a subject of judgement, but not predicate. So, something like the Universal of judgement is constituted. Since, however, the noematic determination is made possible only by the noetic determination, the Universal of self-consciousness envelops, also in rank, the Universal of judgement. In so far, however, as the conscious Self, for its part, is noetically determined, it does not yet contain the world of objects of the transcending noesis; it merely intends it. In a strict sense, the conscious Self contains only that which belongs to inner perception. On the other hand, no noetic determination can be derived from the noematic determination; from the determination of the Universal of judgement, no consciousness can be derived. But, in so far as knowledge, in the strict sense, is constituted by the determination of the Universal of judgement, and is only to be thought of in relation to it, a further and wider concept of "knowing" must be thought of in analogy to the Universal of judgement. Just because of this relationship, I started from the Universal of judgement, and proceeded from there.

The fact that the Universal of judgement has in itself

124

objectivity as truth, and that it contains the object in itself, means that the Universal of judgement is already the noematic determination within the intelligible Universal. Seen in this way, the transition to an enveloping Universal is already contained in the Universal of judgement. The Universal of judgement appears when the Self is reduced to substance, and the intelligible Universal shrinks noematically.

Speaking of an intelligible world, one often imagines a heavenly world which has transcended our real world; the reason for this is that one usually thinks of the world of ideas merely through noematic transcendence. But as free personalities we are actually living in the intelligible world. Seen from this point of view, the so-called real world is nothing else but the world, regarded abstractly.

As has been shown above, the intelligible Universal contains in itself the Universal of self-consciousness, and further the Universal of judgement. But the intelligible Universal is not yet the last one. Although it transcends the conscious Self, transcendent noema and transcendent noesis still confront each other there [in the intelligible Universal]. Although it has the intellectual intuition as its determination, it does not enclose the very last "being". In that which sees itself, the seeing and the seen confront each other, and so it does not yet truly see itself. That is why the free moral will, the last "being" in the intelligible Universal, contradicts itself. Like the "acting" in the Universal of judgement, and the "will" in the Universal of self-consciousness, so the free moral will, the last

125

"being" which has its place in the intelligible Universal, must transcend itself, and must seek "unity in the contradiction" in a "being" which even stands behind itself [the free will].

Existence of the moral Self means consciousness of one's own imperfection, and an infinite striving towards the ideal. In the degree in which the conscience sharpens, one feels more guilty. To solve this contradiction, and to see the true depth of the Self, means to reach religious salvation. Man comes to know the real bottom of the Self, only by denying himself completely. In this state of mind, there is neither good nor evil. By transcending even the intelligible Self in the direction of noesis, one frees oneself even of the free will. There is no more Self which could sin. Even the idea of the good is the shadow of something that is without form.

8.

In order to clarify religious consciousness, we look back once more to that "being" which has its place in the intelligible Universal. I have said that the intelligible Self sees as its own content the "idea". This pertains to its noematic character. But what is its noetic character? What is the very Self which sees its content?

To transcend in the depth of the conscious Self, and to reach the intelligible Self, means nothing else but to go beyond the world of inner perception, and to enclose the transcendent object; it means that the Self becomes conscious of the object without mediation; this union of subject and object is intellectual intuition. In the depth of the conscious Self, we see the deeper content of ourselves, and finally we see ourselves without mediation. In this form of determination, however, the noesis is still bound to the noema, and has not yet freed itself of the aspect of an "act". The Self is more than act; it is essentially that which has the act, or that which has and encloses acts.

The process by which the Self transcends the Self in the depth of the Self means that the Self is [essentially] free, i.e. free will. To be free means to be not enclosed by the object, but to enclose the object. But when the object is not yet the own content of the Self, as in the case of the consciousness-in-general, there is no truly free Self. The truly free Self must have its own content. (Will without content is no will). The free Self must enclose this content as its own in itself, i.e. it must form the "place" in which the Self "is".

That the transcendent Self sees in itself its own content is "intellectual intuition", intuition of the "idea". The significance of the noetic transcendence of the Self would disappear, if something arbitrary did not remain in that intuition. The intelligible Self which has the idea as its content, sees the idea, and realizes it in reality. But it must also contain in itself the direction towards negation of values, because this reveals the noetic independence of the intelligible Self.[1]

"Evil" is the degeneration and shrinking of the trans-

---

1) Here, Nishida refers to chapter 4 of his treatise "The self-determination of the Universal".

cendental Self to a merely psychological Self. The flesh is not evil but the will towards it is. As long as our Self takes the standpoint of the conscious psychological Self, that which the Self wills is neither good nor evil. An animal is neither good nor evil.

What, then, is the "evil will"? Evil is the will that is arbitrary, negates the idea, and has no goal whatever. If one negates one's own content, and allows oneself to be filled with desires in the realm of consciousness, then the "flesh" is evil. Everything that negates value is visible not in the direction of noema, but in that of noesis, and only when the intelligible Self negates its own content, and allows itself to be filled with the content of the conscious [psychological] Self. (The very possibility of negation of value reveals the intelligible noesis!)

In the intelligible world, that which stands in the direction of noesis is always "not-value". The deeper one sees into one's own Self, the more one is suffering; the suffering soul is the deepest reality in the intelligible world. If the last "being which has its place in the intelligible world" is comprehended in the way shown above, it can be understood that one can transcend this Self, and reach religious consciousness. The Self, transcending itself, sees itself deeper and deeper in the direction of noesis; this is the truly free Self. The free Self sees the bottom of that Self which sees the idea. By regarding the intelligible Self merely as that which sees the idea, the noetic independence of the intelligible Self can not be indicated. The self which sees the idea is still bound to the noema; it is merely universal. The true noetic intelligible Self is essentially individual and free; it is freedom itself.

The conscious will, mirroring its own content on the plane of consciousness, and making its content its object, is conscious of itself, not merely as the intending, but also as the intended. The analogy is true for the intelligible Self: here is something that, on the one side, mirrors its own content, the idea, on the transcendent plane of consciousness, and on the other side, is itself non-ideal, and knows itself to see the idea. Therefore, similar to the contradiction in the will, one must suffer from the contradiction in oneself, the more the deeper one is and the deeper one sees one's own Self. To free oneself of this contradiction, and to see the last basis of one's own Self, is the religious consciousness.

Just as the Self of the "consciousness-in-general" was reached by transcending the conscious will, so one must realize a kind of transcendence, i.e. a "conversion", in order to reach the religious [standpoint]. In this way, we free ourselves of the contradiction in ourselves, and see the deepest basis of our Self, without mediation.

The so-called intelligible character is objectivised freedom. It is nothing else but the shadow of the Self, bound to the noema. By proceeding in the direction of the intelligible character, we miss the [true] Self. We see but its shadow, and the Self suffers the more under its own contradiction.

In the artistic intuition, the noesis submerges into the noema, and the intelligible Self sees the Self determined by the noema; therefore, one is free of the contradiction of the Self, and one feels something that is closely related to religious salvation. But it is still a determined Self, seen through artistic intuition, and not the free Self itself.

Conscience, seeing the free Self itself, is self-contradicting: he who says that he does not need to feel ashamed before his conscience merely confesses that his conscience is dull. He who has a feeling of deep guilt sees himself deepest. The true Self becomes visible, when we reflect deeply in ourselves and heap reflection on reflection, until all reflecting seems to be exhausted. Only he who has sunk into the depth of the consciousness of sin, or only he who sees no more way of penitence can comprehend God's holy love.

The fact that the last which has its place in the intelligible Universal has the contradiction in itself, also means that there is a desire for a transcendence. There must be a transcendence which stands behind it.

Whenever a Universal finds its place in another enveloping Universal, and is "lined" with it, the last "being" which had its place in the enveloped Universal, becomes self-contradictory. According to this, the intelligible Universal can not be the last Universal; there must be a Universal which envelopes even the intelligible Universal; it may be called the place of absolute nothingness. That is the religious consciousness. In the religious consciousness, body and soul disappear, and we unite ourselves with the absolute Nothingness. There is neither "true" nor "false", neither "good" nor "evil". The religious value is the value of negation of value.

It sounds absurd to speak of a value of negation of value, but that which is usually called value is value objectivised in the direction of noema, value which has become a "thing". When one, however, transcends infinitely in the direction of noesis, i.e. if one accepts a value of existence, all in this direction is negation of normative values. When the value of shall-character is negated in such a way, the value of being-character, or the value of existence, ascends and reveals itself.

A deeper reality than substance, which can be subject, but not predicate, was the conscious Self, which negates that objective determination [of substance]. Among the different forms of the conscious Self, the willing Self has the highest value of existence, higher than the theoretical Self.

So-called philosophy of values takes the standpoint of the constitutive subject, and deals with determinations of an objective being. But this philosophy of values, reflecting on itself, has no logical form to determine itself. For that philosophy objective being is always value and no true "being". It is a being which itself belongs to the realm of "Shall". Such a standpoint has no possibility of determining true being, nor of discussing something like the "value of existence".

I, on the contrary, take the standpoint of knowledge as "self-determination of the Universal". I think that the "place" or the abstract transcendental plane of determination forms the background of the concrete Universal, determining itself. Then, [in the case of transcending], this "place" is "lined" by an enveloping Universal, and has its "being" therein. Now, the immediate determination of the "place" is the mediated determination of the being, or the form of determination of being [the form of the form]. When, e.g., the Universal of judgement is enveloped by the Universal of self-consciousness, the transcendental plane of predicates becomes the plane of consciousness. That which has its place in this plane of consciousness, i.e. that which "is" here, becomes the direct and immediate determination of the place, when seen from the earlier standpoint of the Universal of judgement; therefore, still seen from that standpoint, it is thought as mere "being" and as "irrational". (This is in analogy to the determination as terminus minor, in the Universal of conclusion.) If the self-determination of the transcendental plane of predicates is called "knowledge", then it can be said that the known determines the knowing.

The same is true in the case when the Universal of self-consciousness is enveloped by the intelligible Universal, and "is" here. The place of the Universal of self-consciousness, i.e. the transcendental plane of consciousness, is the abstract plane of determination, where the [intelligible] Universal determines itself. That which has its place in this plane of determination, is seen as content of the free will, and as arbitrary, from the [earlier] standpoint of the Universal of self-consciousness. This freedom indicates the "reality" of the Self, and from here, self-consciousness itself is "given".

Therefore, the "arbitrary" has deeper reality than the "irrational". In so far as the direct determination of the "place" deepens more and more, the value of existence ascends. I call "value of existence" that value which, contrary to objective knowledge, becomes visible in the direction of the Self, reflecting on itself. In this sense, the last "being" in the intelligible Universal, i.e. "he who has lost his way", in so far as he has his place also in the "place" for the intelligible Universal, is, therefore, the most real. Real, in the deepest sense, as far as it can be methodically determined. The sinner who has lost his way is nearest to God, nearer than the angels.

As content of the intelligible Self, there is noematically no higher value visible than truth, beauty, and the good. In so far, however, as the intelligible Universal is "lined" with the Universal of absolute Nothingness, the "lost Self" becomes visible, and there remains only the proceeding in the direction of noesis. In transcending in that direction the highest value of negation of values becomes visible: it is the religious value. The religious value, therefore, means absolute negation of the Self. The religious ideal consists in becoming a being which denies itself. There is a seeing without a seeing one, and a hearing without a hearing one. This is salvation.

Windelband, in his essay "The Holy" ("Das Heilige"), says that there is no content of value besides that of truth, beauty, and the good. Religious value, he says, can only be found in the fundamental relation between these three forms of consciousness of value, i.e. in the antinomy of the consciousness ("Antinomie des Bewusstseins"). Religious consciousness, according to

Windelband, is the metaphysical reality of the conscious-ness of value, or the consciousness of norm, revealed by the conscience. In short, the religious feeling is the feeling for the reality of the highest value.

I think that, in this way, not only is the value of truth, of beauty, and of the good most intensified, but that there can be derived no specific religious value. No character of value can be derived from reality. The value of existence has its character as value only from the value which existence has in itself. If existence has a value, different from that of truth, of beauty, and of the good, then this means a value of specific character.

9.

I hope to have clarified the standpoint of religious consciousness by what has been said. In the case of the intelligible world, which has its place in the intelligible Universal, noesis and noema still confront each other. The Universal, as determined noematically, is still a determined Universal. The last "being" which has its place there, still contains a contradiction in itself. There-fore, with regard to this Universal, it can not yet be said that it truly envelops the "last". In such a world, the very basis of the true Self does not have its place. There must be something that transcends even that [intelligible] world. That which envelops even the intel-ligible Universal, and which serves as "place" for our true Self, may be called the "place of absolute Nothingness". It is the religious consciousness.

The Universal of judgement is the fundamental form of determination of knowledge. Also intentionality of consciousness, as transcendence in the direction of the predicate, still has logical significance; that which has become conscious is content of knowledge through judgements. Of the intellectual intuition, too, it can be said that it is related to knowledge through concepts, because it has not yet given up [the element of] intentionality. But when it comes to transcending even that intellectual intuition, and when that which has its place in absolute Nothingness is conceived, no more statement can be made with regard to this; it has completely transcended the standpoint of knowledge, and may perhaps be called "world of mystic intuition", unapproachable by word or thinking.

Knowledge through concepts is constituted by a Universal being determined, or by a knowing directly determining a knowing; knowledge is essentially absolute noetic transcendence. (The universal concept is the determined Self.) This direction of noesis may be called "intuition" or "experience", and at its boundary "religious consciousness" reveals itself. Now, it has become impossible to discuss the determination of the content of religious consciousness; in analogy to the determination of the Universal of judgement, such determination exists only in the act of religious "experience". As determination by the Universal of absolute Nothingness, it is a determination without mediation by concept. In a strict sense, everything that has been called above "irrational" and "free", has its very foundation here, where the last "being" is determined. Of the content of religious consciousness, nothing can be said, except that it is "experience".

Always, when a Universal finds its place in another Universal, and is enveloped by that Universal, the transcendental "place" of the enveloped Universal becomes the abstract plane of determination for the enveloping Universal; i.e. it becomes the place where the enveloping Universal mirrors its image. For instance: when the Universal of self-consciousness found its place in the intelligible Universal, a plane of consciousness of the "consciousness-in-general" could be thought of. In the same sense, the intelligible world has its place in the consciousness of God, when the intelligible Universal finds its place in that which was called the "Universal of absolute Nothingness", and is enveloped by that Universal. God, by analogy to the "consciousness-in-general", is the transcendent subject of the intelligible world. And just as the empirical world is constituted by the synthetic unity of the consciousness-in-general, so the intelligible world is thought to be created and ruled by God. In such a way, the religious aspect of the world is established. Just as the transcendental subject of the consciousness-in-general was thought of by transcending the psychological Self, so God is that transcendental subject which is revealed by the noetic transcendence of the intelligible world. That is why even the intelligible Self must kneel before God, as the absolute unity of truth, beauty, and the good. That is the reason

136

why the religious feeling is thought to be the feeling of absolute devotion. It is only through absolute negation of the Self that it becomes possible "to live in God".

Such an aspect of religion, however, is, in my opinion, not deep enough. Just as the intelligible Self, as consciousness-in-general, does not yet have its own content, so this aspect of religion has not yet reached true religious intuition. It is still bound to the intelligible world, where it has its origin. If one is really overwhelmed by the consciousness of absolute Nothingness, there is neither "Me" nor "God"; but just because there is absolute Nothingness, the mountain is mountain, and the water is water, and the being is as it is. The poet says:

> "From the cliff,
> Eight times ten thousand feet high,
> Withdrawing your hand,—
> Flames spring from the plough,
> World burns,
> Body becomes ashes and dirt,
> And resurrects.
> The rice-rows
> Are as ever,
> And the rice-ears
> Stand high".[1]

After having clarified the religious standpoint, I would like to add, finally, a few words about the philosophical standpoint.

The religious standpoint has essentially and completely transcended our knowledge as it is known through

137

concepts. With regard to the landscape of religion, religious experience alone has the last word. Understanding "knowledge" as self-determination of the Universal, and pushing this idea as far as to the Universal of absolute Nothingness, this last Universal is beyond all determination, but there remains still the significance of "mirroring", in so far as it is the "place" of absolute Nothingness. And this mirroring has become the essence of our knowledge. Finally, our soul is thought of as a pure mirror. Something like this was intended by Jakob Böhme, when he said: "So denn der erste Wille ein Ungrund ist, zu achten als ein ewig Nichts, so erkennen wir ihn gleich einem Spiegel, darin einer sein eigen Bildnis sieht, gleich einem Leben" (*Sex Puncta Theosophica*)—"Since the first will is bottomless, like eternal Nothingness, we perceive it as a mirror, in which one sees one's own image as a life". From this standpoint of knowledge which has transcended all knowledge, pure philosophy tries to clarify the different standpoints of

---

1) According to Nishida's personal interpretation, this means:
  The master has given a problem for Zen-meditation, and you are labouring to solve the problems of being, as the farmer over there, on top of the high cliff, is labouring to plough his field. You are hanging on the usual way of thinking like somebody who is hanging on an infinitely high cliff, afraid of falling into the abyss. Withdraw your hand! And see: From the farmer's plough spring sparks,— and you, while the experience of Nothingness springs from your labouring thinking, find "satori", enlightenment. The Universe has become nothing, and the Ego has become nothing. But in the same spark of Nothingness, you regain the world and yourself in wonderful self-identity. In the experience of Nothingness, everything is as it is: the rice-rows are as ever, and the rice-ears stand high. (The author of this poem is the Japanese Zen-Buddhist Kanemitsu Kogun).

knowledge and their specific structures. From the standpoint of the Universal of absolute Nothingness, philosophy tries to clarify the specific "determination" of each enveloped Universal.

Self-determination of the Universal may be called "reason" in the widest sense of the word. Then, philosophy is self-reflection of reason. A peculiar case of such self-reflection is Kant's critical philosophy. In the religious experience as such, however, there does not remain even the meaning of "mirroring". Since I am looking at religion from the standpoint of philosophy, I call religion the standpoint of absolute Nothingness. It is from this philosophical standpoint that I say religion should be thought of in such a way. Here is the point where religion and philosophy touch each other.

The philosophical viewpoint, as one of knowledge, is essentially abstract, compared with art and ethics. But since philosophy has transcended the standpoint of the intelligible Self, it has already transcended art and ethics, and even the religious aspect of life. The religious aspect, as has been said above, is reached in the Universal of absolute Nothingness, and it was there compared with the standpoint of "consciousness-in-general". The philosophical standpoint is that of self-reflection of the religious Self in itself, not looking back on the intelligible world from the religious standpoint, and not making the content of the intelligible world its own content. It is not the standpoint where an absolute Self constitutes the world, but that of self-reflection, or of self-reflection of the absolute Self. Philosophy is only in such a manner

139

occupied with the origin and the structure of knowledge. Critical philosophy, too, is not realized by the consciousness-in-general, but by reflection on it.

The "place" of a Universal is undeterminable [from its own standpoint], and this means that behind it something self-conscious becomes evident. The self-conscious, reflecting on itself, is increasingly self-determining; it determines its own content. In the Universal of self-consciousness, the self-conscious, reflecting on itself, and determining its own content, sees the content of the "concrete Self". The analogy is true for the intelligible Self. But, transcending the intelligible Self, the Universal becomes absolutely undeterminable. At the same time there remains, as content of the conscious Self, which [still] has its place here, the mere form of determination of the Self; one is conscious only of self-consciousness, and knowledge reflects only on knowledge. The so-called religious world-aspect is nothing else but the content of the intelligible world, seen from the point of view of the religious Self. It is not the content of religious self-reflection as such.

When it comes to the religious standpoint, the conscious Self disappears, and so does all content which was intended by it. In the direction of self-determination of knowledge, there remains only formal self-consciousness, i.e. there remains only the primary form ("Urform") of knowledge. This phase of consciousness of absolute Nothingness, which is Nothing as well as Being, can become evident for the theoretical Self, only in self-reflection of knowledge as such. And this is the standpoint of philosophy.

It has been my intention to clarify, from the point of view of consistent criticism, the origin of knowledge, to refer the different kinds of knowledge to their specific standpoints and to their specific values, and to clear up their relations and their order of rank. It can not be denied that Kant's criticism still has something dogmatic in its starting point. If metaphysics, as was said above, consists in discussing the intelligible "being" or existence, I would be ready to justify it. What is wrong in so-called metaphysics is, in my opinion, the fact that it does not clear up the different kinds of knowledge, and confuses the significance of different kinds of "being".

II. GOETHE'S METAPHYSICAL BACKGROUND

by KITARO NISHIDA

Time is a flowing, from eternal past to eternal future. Time is, so to say, born in eternity, and disappears in eternity. Everything revealed in history, has its form and figure on such a background of eternity. Seen from the point of view of history, everything is connected according to cause and effect, and flows from eternal past into eternal future.

But time, as self-determination of the eternal "Now", is essentially contained in this Now. There where time is, contained and extinguished, personality appears, as content of eternity.

This is true for all forms of civilization, but art is especially something formed by history on the background of eternity. Just as Michelangelo's unfinished sculptures, or the sculptures of Rodin are hewn out of a massive block of marble, so is all great art a relief, cut out of the marble of eternity.

This may appear as something impersonal, compared with the particular element, but it is not something that, like matter, is the opposite of form. It is but in this [background] and through it, that something personal has been formed. Without such a background, there is nothing personal whatever.

Michelangelo's block of marble is not mere matter; it is, in itself, already an essential part of art. Just as our mind sees itself in itself, the personal is an image of eternity, mirrored in eternity.

Any kind of art has essentially such a background, and that which does not have such a background, can not be called art. According to the varying relationship between this background and that which has been formed in it, different personal content is visible, and different artistic content is formed there.

Oriental art is essentially impersonal because the background is an integral part of it. This produces [in our hearts] a formless, boundless vibration, and an endless, voiceless echo.

Western art, however, is formed through and through. In Greece, where the "eidos" was thought to be the true "being", plastic art is so completely formed that it would be impossible to add to its beauty of form. Still, we have the feeling that some kind of depth was somehow lacking in Greek art. Eternity, in the Greek sense, stands before us as something visible, and does not embrace us from the back of things.

In Christian culture, where the personal [element] is recognized as true "being", art gains in depth and background. Early Christian art has an inwardness, which reminds us of Buddhist paintings in the East. Later, in the art of Michelangelo, there is such great vigour, that we have the feeling of standing in front of a deep crater's turbulent black flames. His art has a powerful depth and a colossal background.

What is it that forms the background in Goethe's poetry? Out of what kind of marble-block is his art cut?

If one imagines the background of eternity as space, one can distinguish a two-dimensional and a three-dimensional

146

background, a formless one, and a formed one. And with regard to the background of three dimensions, one can distinguish height and depth. Then, the background of the plastic art of Michelangelo must be called "deep"; in his art there is a vigorous force rising from the depth of an abyss. On the other hand, one feels in Dante's "Divina Commedia" a height to which one must look up; in this background, there is the transcendent Christian God.

The background of Goethe's poetry is not three-dimensional; it can be imagined as two-dimensional, and can be called formless [i.e. without form or figure].

Of Eastern paintings we use terms like "high-wide", "deep-wide", and "plane-wide"; but that which I have called "two-dimensional" is height without height, depth without depth, and width without width.

Such an art which has in its background something that extends infinitely without form, is in danger of negating the human element. The infinite which merely denies the finite, is imagined as dark fate, incompatable with humanity. But that which forms the background of Goethe's poetry is not such a two-dimentional background; [on the contrary], there is everywhere something that encloses the human element, and nothing that denies it. Humanity is quasi-dissolved in this background. But this "dissolving" does not mean a loss of individuality. The sound of true human individuality is to be heard only where there is such a background. This background is like a "Resonanzboden"[1] of humanity.

---

1) Nishida uses in the original this German word for soundboard.

Could it not be said that the background of
Rembrandt's paintings has such a significance? There
is depth in his paintings, but it is a completely different
type of depth, compared with Michelangelo; it is not
force, but softness, it is not the depth of force, but the
depth of feeling. Verhaeren says at the end of his
book "Rembrandt" (p. 120): "Il recueille les pleurs,
les cris, les joies, les souffrances, les espoirs au plus intime
de nous-mêmes et nous montre le Dieu qu'il célèbre,
agité des mêmes tumultes que nous". This God is
something like a sounding board of humanity. Speaking
of soft depth, one might be reminded of Leonardo da
Vinci, but Leonardo is intellectual; the smile of Mona
Lisa is mysterious, but it is not the smile of love.

The relationship between Goethe and the philosophy
of Spinoza is well known. Goethe narrates how he, in
his early youth, kneeled before the throne of Nature.
After having read Spinoza's "Ethica", he was charmed by
the doctrine, and never gave it up throughout his life.
Goethe thought of all as one, and nature as God, and his
rather contemplative philosophy of life was based on this.
So he has a fundamental tone in common with Spinoza's
pantheism. But Goethe was less a Spinozist than he
himself believed, and less than many have said since.
From a different point of view, one could even say that
he took the opposite standpoint. In Spinoza's philosophy,
eternity is two-dimensional, but negating the individual.
Spinoza's "substantia" negates the individual completely.
In his philosophy, the individual is merely a "modus"
of the "substantia". There is nothing like "time", and

his philosophy does not allow for anything like individuality. Spinoza's "natura" is a nature of mathematical
necessity. Though he negated the Jewish theism, his
Jewish peculiarity is shown by his monism, and in the
consistency of his strict logic.

On the other hand, Goethe's pantheism encloses individuality everywhere. Nature, in Goethe's sense, does
not deny individuality, but produces something individual
everywhere. This nature is like an infinite space which,
itself formless, produces form everywhere. Like the
moonlight in "An den Mond", like the sea in "Der
Fischer", and like the mist in "Erlkönig", Goethe's
"nature" is essentially something that harmonizes with
our heart.

> "River! flow along vale
> Without rest or peace,
> Murmur to my silent tale
> Whispering melodies!"[1)]

There is "Mitklingen"[2)] in the very depth of our soul.

While Spinoza's "nature" is essentially mathematical,
Goethe's "nature" may well be called artistic. While
Spinoza is Jewish, Goethe may well be called Christian,
especially a Christan South-German. Goethe whose long
life of more than eighty years was completely given to
the joy and pain of emotion, was totally different from

---

1) "Rausch, Fluss, das Tal entlang,
   Ohne Rast und Ruh',
   Rausche, flüstre meinem Sang
   Melodien zu!"

2) German in the original.

149

Spinoza, whose life was spent in his room in loneliness, while thinking and polishing lenses.

Goethe is similar to Leibniz, in as far as he, too, emphasized individuality. He agreed with Leibniz's "monad", and with Aristotle's concept of "entelechy". Unlike Leibniz's "windowless monad", Goethe's "monad" makes its sound and fades boundlessly away into the distances of eternity.

All this must be the reason why Goethe, despite his various talents and manifold activities, was the greatest lyrical poet. In the field of drama, where form and figure is essential, the background must be three-dimensional; only with regard to lyrics does one not know from where it comes, and to where it goes. It is an overflow of the spring of life. There is nobody but Goethe in whom personal experience has become poetry so directly. He sings:

> "All in life repeats again,
> Joy and woe becomes refrain".[1]

So his poetry is the immediate expression of his unusual experiences. He himself confesses in the poem "An die Günstigen":

> "None confession like in prosa;
> But we oft confess sub rosa
> In the Muses' silent grove.
> . . . .
> How I erred, and how I strived,

---

1) "Spät erklingt, was früh erklang,
    Glück und Unglück wird Gesang".

What I suffered, how I lived,
Flow'rets in a bunch are here".[1]
And his Tasso says: "Und wenn der Mensch verstummt
in seiner Qual, gab mir ein Gott, zu sagen, was ich leide".
It is his lyrical poetry, which touches us the deepest.
Lyrical art is the formless voice of life.

It needs no saying, that poetry is originally and
essentially a product of intuition, and that intuition is
the essence of the poet. This is especially true of Goethe.
To him, all being becomes the object of intuition. He
warns the physicist: "Natur hat weder Kern noch
Schale; alles ist sie mit einem Male". And in
"Epirrhema" he says:

"Students of nature, make this your goal:
Heed the specimen, heed the Whole;
Nothing is inside or out,
What's within must outward sprout".[2]

Even his biological studies, and his theory of colours,
though scientific research, are based on the vigour of
his artistic intuition. In this there is a touch of Platonism,
one might say, Already in his youth in Strassburg

---

1) "Niemand beichtet gern in Prosa,
   Doch vertraun wir oft sub rosa
   In der Musen stillem Hain.
   . . . .
   Was ich irrte, was ich strebte,
   Was ich litt, und was ich lebte,
   Sind hier Blumen nur im Strauss".

2) "Müsset im Naturbetrachten
   Immer eins wie alles achten;
   Nichts ist drinnen, nichts ist draussen;
   Denn was innen, das ist aussen".

Goethe had a longing for Raffael and classical antiquity, but his Italian voyage, as everybody knows, had the greatest influence on his art. This is obvious from the difference between "Tasso" or "Iphigenie", and "Götz" or "Werther". And is there not something in his concepts of "Urtier" and "Urpflanze" that reminds us of Plato's "idea"?

In the second part of "Faust", Faust must descend to the realm of the "mothers" in order to be able to conjure Helena. The beautiful Helena-scenes show Goethe's longing for the classical world, and are necessary stages of Faust's development in his continued endeavour towards, a higher existence. But it was merely a stage, not the goal. When Faust embraced Helena, only her veil and robe remained in his hands. He returned home and turned to an active life for the benefit of society. Goethe was thoroughly Germanic in his essence. The Goethe who wrote the second part of "Faust" and the "Wanderjahre", was still the author of "Götz" and "Werther". Although he was touched and refined by the spirit of the classical world, in the depth of his soul there was not the clarity of "eidos", but a depth of feeling, to which the vision of ideas was not sufficient.

Mere feeling tends towards mysticism, but Goethe was not Novalis. In Goethe, eidos is heart, and heart is eidos. There is no inside or outside; everything is an "open secret". Moreover, and above all else, Goethe's ideal was, as shown by the second part of "Faust" and by the "Wanderjahre", action for the community of men. Faust's last words are:

"Then might I say, that moment seeing:
Ah, linger on, thou art so fair!
The traces of my earthly being
Can perish not in aeons — they are here"[1]

In the beginning of the drama "Faust", God says: "Es irrt der Mensch, solang er strebt", and at the end, the angels say: "Wer immer strebend sich bemüht, den können wir erlösen". Goethe, the great poet, was not striving for enjoyment of beauty, but for earnest endeavour in life.

Prometheus shouted:
"Cover thy spacious heaven, Zeus!
With clouds of mist,
. . . .
Thou must my earth
let standing here.
. . . .
I know nought poorer
Under the sun than ye gods!"[2]

And he finishes with the same vigour of life:

---

1) "Zum Augenblicke dürft' ich sagen:
Verweile doch, du bist so schön!
Es kann die Spur von meinen Erdetagen
Nicht in Aeonen untergehn".

2) "Bedecke deinen Himmel, Zeus,
Mit Wolkendunst
. . . .
Musst mir meine Erde
Doch lassen stehn
. . . .
Ich kenne nichts Aermeres
Unter der Sonn' als euch, Götter!"

"Here sit I, forming mortals
After my image; a race, resembling me,
To suffer, to weep,
To enjoy, to be glad,
And thee to scorn,
as I".[1]

In Goethe himself there was originally something Prometheus-like, something Titanic. His whole life was a life of noble action. He lets Faust say: "Werd ich beruhigt je mich auf ein Faulbett legen, so sei es gleich um mich getan!" Even Goethe's "resignation" ("Entsagung") was an active one. Man can find salvation only by acting.

In this respect, Goethe reminds us of Fichte, who called indolence the hereditary sin of man. But in the depth of his personality, there was nature, and not moral obligation:

"The blind desire, the impatient will,
The restless thoughts and planes are still;
We yield ourselves—and wake in bliss".[2]

Here is something that reminds us of the English poet

---

1)   "Hier sitz' ich, forme Menschen
     Nach meinem Bilde,
     Ein Geschlecht, das mir gleich sei:
     Zu leiden, zu weinen,
     Zu geniessen und zu freuen sich—
     Und dein nicht zu achten,
     Wie ich".

2)   "statt heissem Wünschen, wildem Wollen,
     Statt läst'gem Fordern, strengem Sollen
     Sich aufzugeben ist Genuss".
                          Eins und Alles.

Browning:

> "The year's at the spring
> And day's at the morn;
> Morning's at seven;
> The hill-side's dew-pearled;
> The lark's on the wing;
> The snail's on the thorn:
> God's in his heaven—
> All's right with the world!"

Browning's last words were:

> "One who never turned his back but marched
> breast forward,
>
> Never doubted clouds would break,
>
> Never dreamed, though right were worsted, wrong
> would triumph,
>
> Held we fall to rise, are baffled to fight better,
>
> Sleep to wake".

However, that which stands behind Goethe is not the same as in the case of Browning. That which is standing behind Goethe encloses action, is salvation. In the background of the Promethean Goethe glitters the moonlight:

> Bush and vale thou fill'st again
> With thy misty ray;
> And my spirit's heavy chain
> Castest far away.
> Thou doest o'er my fields extend
> Thy sweet soothing eye;

155

> Watching like a gentle friend
> O'er my destiny".[1]

In this background whispers a friend's voice, narrating what wanders through the labyrinth of our hearts, unknown to man. And in "Faust" the "chorus mysticus" reveals Goethe's metaphysical background, in saying:

> "All earth comprises
> Is symbol alone;
> What there ne'er suffices
> As fact here is known;
> All past the humanly
> Wrought here in love;
> The Eternal-Womanly
> Draws us above".[2]

It is not an eternal Male, as in the case of Browning, but the eternal Female.

---

1)   "Füllest wieder Busch und Tal
     Still mit Nebelglanz,
     Lösest endlich auch einmal
     Meine Seele ganz;
     Breitest über mein Gefild
     Lindernd deinen Blick,
     Wie des Freundes Auge mild
     Über mein Geschick".

2)   "Alles Vergängliche
     Ist nur ein Gleichnis;
     Das Unzulängliche,
     Hier wird's Ereignis;
     Das Unbeschreibliche,
     Hier ist's getan;
     Das Ewig-Weibliche
     Zieht uns hinan".

Goethe's universalism does not, like Spinoza's, reduce everything to the one substance, denying man; he sees all things in man. And still, each thing is not a substance, and indestructable as in Leibniz's monadology. According to his words "Im Grenzenlosen sich zu finden, wird gern der Einzelne verschwinden" ("The individual will willingly disappear, in order to find itself in the Infinite") the individuals are absorbed in the Universe, without any pre-established harmony between them. When Goethe says in the second part of "Faust": "Am farbigen Abglanz haben wir das Leben" ("We have life in its colourful resplendence!"), there is something of Platonism, but since he is Germanic, his world is a world of action, and not a world of intuition. Resignation is resignation through action. In the depth of this world of action is salvation, and not, as in the case of Kant or Fichte, moral obligation. According to the words "enträtselnd sich den ewig Ungenannten" ("solving for himself the riddle of the eternally Unnamed") in the Marienbad Elegy, there is something like a friend's eye, or a friend's voice, consoling our soul. But still, figure and form do not disappear in the rhythm of emotion, as in Novalis. For Goethe, there is no inward and no outward; everything is as it is; it comes from where there is nothing, and goes where there is nothing.

And just in this coming from nothingness and going into nothingness there is the gentle sound of humanity.

Yes, Goethe's universalism is just the opposite of that of Spinoza. His philosophy of life, based on this kind of universalism, does not remind us of the intellectual

157

love of the Stoic sage, but of the love of Maria, the Eternal-Womanly.

Verhaeren said that the medieval man wanted to come nearer to God by "naiveté" and "candeur", but Rembrandt by "souffrance", "angoisse", "tendresse", and "joie", i.e. by a full human life. Is it not the same with Goethe? In this, he ressembles Rembrandt more than Spinoza. Proceeding in this direction, we reach something like an art of sadness without the shadow of sadness, an art of joy without the shadow of joy, as we see it in the art of the East.

To Goethe the man, who sought liberation from Werther's sufferings, Rome gave the "Roman Elegies"; to the old Goethe, who sought liberation from reality, the Orient gave the "West-Östlichen Divan".

History is not only flowing from the past into the future; true history is a counterflow to the movement from the future into the past; it is eternal rotation in the "now".

When history is regarded as extinguished in the eternal past, something like the Greek civilization appears, and it takes everything as a shadow of eternity. On the other hand, when history is regarded as going to, and disappearing in the eternal future, something like the Christian civilization appears, and it takes everything as a road to eternity. When, however, history is thought of as determination in the eternal Now, where past and future are extinguished in the present, then everything comes without a whence in its coming, and goes without a whither in its going, and that which is, is eternally what it is. Such a thinking flows in the depth of the civilization of the East, in which we have grown up.

(Written in December 1931).

III. THE UNITY OF OPPOSITES

by KITARO NISHIDA

1.

The world of reality is a world where things are acting on things. The form and figure of reality are to be thought as a mutual relationship of things, as a result of acting and counteracting. But this mutual acting of things means that things deny themselves, and that the thing-character is lost.

Things forming one world, by acting on each other, means that they are thought as parts of one world. For instance, things acting on each other in space, means that things have a spatial character. When it comes to "space" in the exact sense of physics, "forces" are thought as changes in space.

But when things are thought as parts of one whole, it means that the concept of acting things is lost, that the world becomes static and that reality is lost. The world of reality is essentially the one as well as the many; it is essentially a world of the mutual determination of single beings.

That is why I call the world of reality "absolute contradictory self-identity" [or "unity of opposites"].

Such a world essentially moves from the formed, the product, to the forming, the creative production.

The world does not — as according to traditional physics — consist in mutual acting and counteracting of unchangeable atoms, i.e. not as the [mechanical] one of the many, for if such were the case, the world would be nothing else than an [eternal] repetition of the same world. It is equally impossible to think it as teleological unfolding of the whole one. If it were so, single beings could not act on single beings. World can not be thought [only] as the one of the many, or [only] as the many of the one. It is essentially a world, where the data are something formed, i.e. dialectically given, and which negates itself, [moving] slowly from the formed to the forming. It is impossible to think either the one whole, or the many single beings, as substratum in the depth of this world. It is a creative world, phenomenon as well as reality, moving by itself.

That which "is" in reality, is, as determined, through and through "being", and as formed, through and through changing and passing away. It can be said that it is Being as well as Nothingness. Therefore, I have spoken in other places of the world of absolute Nothingness, and I have called it, as a world of endless moving, the world of determination without a determining one.

In the world described here as "unity of opposites", the present itself necessarily determines the present. This world is neither determined by the past through cause and effect, nor by the future, teleologically, i.e. it is neither the one of the many, nor the many of the one. Time is, in the end, neither to be thought from the past, nor from the future. If the present is regarded merely as the moment, as a point on a continuous straight line, then there is no present whatever, and, consequently, no time at all. [The reason for this] is that the past has passed, and yet has not passed in the present. Further-

164

more, the future has not yet come although it shows itself in the present, since past and future are confronting each other as unity of opposites, this being the stuff out of which time is constituted. And, as unity in contradiction, time moves endlessly from past to future, from the formed to the forming. Although the moment must be thought as a point on a straight line, time is constituted as discontinous continuity, just as Plato stated that the moment was outside time. It can be said that time constitutes itself through absolute contradictory self-identity of the one and the many.

The concrete present is essentially the coexistence of innumerable moments, the one of the many. It is quasi a space of time. Here, the moments of time are negated, but the one which denies the many, is itself the contradiction. The fact that the moments are negated means that time itself gets lost, and that the present disappears. If that is so, — are the moments of time constituted singly and discontinuously? But then, time itself would be impossible, and with it the moments would disappear. Time consists essentially in the present coexistence of moments. By saying this I mean that time, as the one of the many as well as the many of the one, consists in the contradictory unity of the present. This, too, is the reason why I say that the present itself determines the present, and that in this way time is constituted.

Touching eternity in a moment of time, the Now, means nothing else than this: that the moment, in becoming a "true" moment, becomes one of the individual many, which is to say, the moment of the eternal present which is the unity of opposites. Seen from the other side, this means nothing else than that time is constituted as the self-determination of the eternal now.

The fact that in the present the past has passed and not yet passed, and the future has not yet come and yet shows itself, means not only, as it is thought in abstract logic, that the past is connected with the future, or becomes one with it; it also means that they become one, by negating each other, and the point, where future and past, negating each other, are one, is the present. Past and future are confronting each other, as the dialectical unity of the present. Just because they are the unity of opposites, past and future are never connected, and there is an eternal movement from the past into the future.

In so far as the present is the unity of the one and the many, as well as of the many and the one, and in so far as the present is a space of time, a "form" is necessarily decided, and time is destroyed. Here, eternity is touched, transcending time; because the present in time is the self-determination of the eternal now. But this present, as unity of opposites, is decided as something which is to be negated, and time moves on, from one present to another present.

That the one is the one of the many, indicates space-character; the mechanism has the form: from the many towards the one; it means movement from the past into the future. On the contrary, the fact that the many are the many of the one means the dynamic time-character

166

of the world; purpose and evolution have the form: from the one towards the many; it means movement from the future into the past. The world as unity of opposites, from the formed towards the forming, is essentially a world from present to present.

Reality has form and figure. That which "is" really, is something decided, i.e. reality; at the same time, because it has been decided through unity of opposites, it is moving through the inner contradiction of reality itself. Behind it, there is neither the one nor the many. The fact of decision, [i.e. the very fact that form and figure are decided] is necessarily contradictory in itself.

Such a world, as unity of opposites, from the formed towards the forming, is essentially a world of "poiesis". Ordinarily, in speaking of creative action, we have only in mind that someone makes something. But in saying that a thing, however artificial, objectively comes into existence, one must recognize that it [i.e. the creative action] is objective, too. Since we have hands, we can make and form things. Our hands are the result of an evolution of thousands of years; they are· from the formed towards the forming. Aristotle says — although metaphorically — "nature creates". Of course, this does not mean that our creating is merely the activity of nature. And, of course, it is not merely our hands that create.

What does it mean: making things? Creating things? It means: changing the composition of things. An architect, making a house, changes the composition and relations of things, according to their qualities; i.e. he changes their form. (This is possible in a world of

167

"composé", like that of Leibniz). The world of reality essentially has form; it has been decided as the one of the many. But if the world is thought completely in this way, from the many towards the one, [i.e. mechanically], there is no room for anything like creative action. If, however, the world is thought, on the other hand, as from the one towards the many, then it is necessarily teleological, a world of living beings, where there is only the activity of nature.

At the base of the world, there are neither the many nor the one; it is a world of absolute unity of opposites, where the many and the one deny each other. There is the individual, as individual, "form-giving". The individual creates, makes things, and is, at the same time: from the formed towards the forming (i.e. it is in the transitory movement from being a formed individual towards becoming a forming individual]. This is the creative activity of the "historical nature". Time, being fundamentally but one time, is constituted through self-determination of the present, which, as space-of-time, is from present to present. In analogy, the character of the world as "from the formed towards the forming" means, as unity of opposites, the creativeness of the individual, on the other hand, the creative action of the individual means. the world is from the formed towards the forming. The fact that man is "homo faber" means· the world is "historical". On the other hand, the historical character of the world means: man is "homo faber".

In the world of unity of opposites, we are touching

in the present moment of time something that has transcended time. So in the world "from the formed towards the forming", in the world of the "homo faber", there is always form visible in reality. It is peculiar for this world that the line from the past to the future is vertically cut by the plane of consciousness. The world from the formed towards the forming has a plane of consciousness which has the significance of "mirroring". Creation is essentially conscious; we create "acting-reflecting". In the plane of consciousness in the world of unity of opposites, there is the creating Self, thinking and free. Out of the creating [action] rises our individual self-consciousness.

It must be difficult to understand for many that I mean the world of reality by saying that in the depth of the world there are neither one nor many, and that through mutual negation of the one and the many the world is from the formed towards the forming. Speaking of reality, most people suppose the many as basis of the world, and they think an atomistic world of causal necessity, or a world of matter.

Of course, the world of unity of opposites is, on the one hand, actually to be thought in such a manner. Under the perspective of unity of opposites of reality, the world must be thought so. But reality is more than mere given data. What is given, is "formed". Reality is where we "are" and "act". Acting is not mere will; it is "forming", it is the making of things.

We are forming things. Things, being formed by us, are, at the same time, independent of us; they are forming us. What is more, our forming itself stems from the world of things.

Reality is that in which we behave acting-reflecting. That is why we usually call reality the place where we are with our body. But reality is there where forming and formed, contradicting each other, are one, and where the present determines the present

Scientific knowledge, too, arises on this standpoint of reality. The world of scientific reality, too, must be comprehended from this point of view. Just as our own body is perceived in its exterior movements (Noiré), so our own Self is perceived through "poiesis" in the historical-social world. The historical-social world is essentially "from the formed towards the forming". Without the social element, there is no "from the formed towards the forming", there is no "poiesis". The standpoint of our thinking is necessarily in the historical-social world.

There are many different opinions with regard to the starting point of philosophy. In Japan, the standpoints of epistemology and that of phenomenology have dominated generally. Seen from these standpoints, that which I am saying here will be regarded as dogmatism. But those standpoints, too, are necessarily historical-social. Today, we must, once more, return to the beginning, and analyse the historical-social world logically-ontologically. That means: we must again start with the beginning of Greek philosophy. Also the standpoint of theory of knowledge, where subject and object confront each other, must be examined critically. Knowledge, too, is a

170

happening in the historical-social world. This does not mean that I would return to the old metaphysics. After Kant, Lotze returned to ontology and examined knowledge from that point of view. But his ontology was not historical-social in our sense.

In the world which is moving by itself, as unity of the opposites of the many and the one, individual and environment always confront each other; it is a world which proceeds by forming itself through contradiction, i.e. it is a world of "life".

By saying that the individual forms the environment, and the environment forms the individual, I do not mean that a form forms a matter. The individual is essentially acting, and determining itself. Action means negation of the other, and means the will to make the other [an expression of] oneself. It means that the Self wants to be the world. But it also means, on the other hand, that the Self denies itself, and becomes a part of the world.

World, thought as world of reality, must be a unity of opposites, in the shown sense, whether it is thought mechanically, as the one of the many, or teleologically, as the many of the one. Even when it is thought mechanically or teleologically, there is not yet room for an individual determining itself. The individual is not yet truly acting. A world of true mutual action must be something like Leibniz' world of monads. The monad, mirroring the world, is, at the same time, one perspective of the world. It is at the same time expression and representation. ("exprimer", "représenter"). And yet,

171

the individual is not [merely] intellectual like the monad; it is essentially forming itself and is essentially expressive. In a world where there is neither the one nor the many to be thought as its basis and in a world which, as unity of opposites, is moving from the formed to the forming, the individual must, essentially, be something that forms itself in the way of expression.

If the individual, as individual of a world of unity of the opposites of the one and the many, is mirroring that world, then the self-determination of the individual is necessarily "desire". The individual acts neither mechanically nor teleologically, but by mirroring the world in its own Self. That I call "conscious". Even the instinct of animals, seen in its essence, must have this quality. Therefore I said that our activity originated from "action-intuition". Because we "see" things, action is realized. "Action-intuition" means: activity, contradicting itself, is contained in the object. The world as unity of the opposites of the many and the one, moving from the formed towards the forming, is essentially acting-reflecting, and the individual is necessarily desiring.

By "form" I do not mean the figure of a static thing, but the activity of forming itself in a world of unity of the opposites of the many and the one, from the formed towards the forming. Plato's "idea", too, must have been essentially something of this kind. There is no desire without seeing things, contradicting oneself, and there is no action without [seen] form.

In animal life, seeing can not be clear; it must be a dreamy seeing of images of things; that is why the

172

animal is said to have only instinct. Animals, according to their nature, can by no means form things outside themselves, even if one allows the possibility of expression. The animal has not yet a world of objects, and it can not be said that it truly acts by "action-intuition". Here is not yet any poiesis. The formed is not yet separated from the forming, and it cannot be said that the formed forms the forming. It is not "from the formed towards the forming". It is a bodily [biological] forming, common to all living beings.

Only when it comes to man, where the Self, as monad, is mirroring the world, and is, at the same time, itself a (viewpoint of) perspective of the world, there is activity through action-intuition, [originating] from seeing things in a world of objects. The standpoint of man's acting is [as it were] a seeing of his Self outside himself. Here, the formed forms the forming, and that is why I say: from the formed towards the forming. Therefore, here is poiesis. Man can be called: historical-bodily [or historical-biological]. But acting from the standpoint of representation being equal to expression, he can also be called: logical-spiritual.

As has been said above, the individual is creative as individual; while forming the world, he is, at the same time, a creative part of the self-forming creative world. This makes the individual an individual. The world, as unity of opposites, from the formed towards the forming, is essentially a world "from form to form". As it has been said above that the present determines the present, so it can be said now that form determines form, ["form"-

173

"Gestalt"]. Seen in this way, the world, as unity of the opposites of the many and the one, is forming itself, it is essentially "formation".

Such self-forming form is the "subject" of the historical world. I call it "historical species". That which I have called "form", is not an abstract static form, separated from reality, and when I say "from form to form" I do not mean a transition without mediation. I mean the form which belongs to reality itself, as unity of the opposites of the many and the one.

Biological phenomena can be reduced to physico-chemical phenomena, but then they become superficial combinations of matter; if they should be recognized as real, they must have some kind of form, and the form of living beings is essentially "functional". Form and function are inseparable in the living being. Form is not merely that which can be seen with our eyes. Also the instinct of animals is form-activity. Human society, too, has essentially its form. Form is "paradigma". We are acting through the form of our species by "action-intuition". We act through seeing, and we see through acting.

The world as unity of opposites, moving infinitely from the formed towards the forming, is, as has been said above, moving from one form to another form, formative in nature, that is, subjective [as acting]. In this world, individuals and environment are confronting each other. The individual forms the environment, and the environment forms the individual.

Environment is not merely material, in a world of

174

unity of absolute contradictions. However, it is essential for the environment that it negates form. Compared with the "from the one to the many", it is essentially "from the many to the one". Negating itself, the individual forms its environment, and the environment, negating itself, forms the individual. This does not mean that form becomes matter, and matter becomes form. Under discussion are neither form and matter, nor differences of formation. Saying: the world is "from the many to the one", means a causal and deterministic interpretation of the world; the world is seen from the past, and thought mechanically. To say: the world is "from the one to the many", is to give a teleological interpretation. Mere teleological interpretation, however, is not free from space-character and not free of determinism, as has been shown in the case of life in the biological sense. If one calls the world truly "from the one to the many", one must think the world as temporal, one must suppose something like Bergson's pure duration. ("durée-pure)

"Truly creative" means: "from the future"; there is no more "from the past"! Where the pure duration negates itself, and where the pure duration, in negating and contradicting itself, has space-character, is the world of reality. In a world of pure duration which can not turn back, even for the length of a moment, there is no "present". But when that which has space-character, and which negates itself, is temporal, i.e. when it, contradicting itself, moves by itself, then and only then is truly the world of reality. Therefore, in the present of the world, which as absolute unity of opposites moves from present to present, subject and environment confront each other; the individual negating itself, forms the environment and vice versa. And the present of the world of reality moves from the direction of that which, as unity of the opposites of individual and environment, and of the one and the many, has already been decided, [it moves] from the formed towards the forming. This is called the movement from the past into the future. The "formed" has already entered the environment and has already become a part of the past. And still, the nothing [proves to be] an ens, and the past, though passed away, a being: contradicting itself, the formed forms the subject [the individual].

By seeing the world only from the many, or only from the one, and by thinking the world only as mechanism, or only teleologically, there is no "from the formed towards the forming". There is no room for something like "formation" [or creation]. But in a world of absolute unity of the many and the one, where the many, negating themselves, are the one, and the one, negating itself, is the many, the forming of the environment by the self-negating individual is, at the same time, on the contrary, the forming of a new individual by the self-negating environment. And the passing of the temporal present into past, means the advance of future.

In the historical world, there is nothing that is merely "given". "Given" is something "formed" which, negating itself, forms the forming. The formed is something that

176

has passed away, and has entered Nothingness. But the very fact that time passes into the past is the birth of future, and the rising of a new subject. In this sense, I am speaking of [that which moves] "from the formed towards the forming".

By saying that in the historical world individual and environment, negating each other, are always confronted, I mean that they are confronted like past and future in the temporal present. And like the present, as unity of opposites, moves from the past into the future, so [the historical world] is the movement from the formed towards the forming. In a world of unity of the opposites of the many and the one, the individual, as a monad, mirrors the world, and is, at the same time, on the contrary, a perspective of the world. Out of that which is formed in such a world, the forming arises, and forms again.

In this way, the world which moves by itself through contradictions, as unity of the opposites of the many and the one, always contradicts itself in the present; the present is the "place" of contradiction. From the standpoint of abstract logic, it is impossible to say that things which contradict each other are connected; they contradict each other just because they can not be connected. But there would be no contradiction if they did not touch each other somewhere. Facing each other is already a synthesis. Here is the dominion of dialectical logic.

The point of contradiction is the temporal "moment". But while the moment can be imagined as outside time,

177

it is also a point in that dialectical "space" where facing-each-other is, at the same time, negation and affirmation. Time, thought abstractly, is imagined as a straight-line flowing from the past into the future. But the real time of the historical world, can be called "principle of formation", or "style of productivity" of the historical world of reality. This means "from the formed towards the forming"; it means "from the past towards the future". The form of the temporal present is form, in the sense of this "style of productivity".

When the same production is repeated because the style of productivity is not creative, time appears as a straight-lined process in the usual sense. The present has no content there; it is a point-of-moment, incomprehensible and without form. In this incomprehensible point-of-moment, past and future should be connected. The time of physics is of this kind. In the physical world there is nothing creative; there is [nothing] but eternal repetition of the same world. There is a world of space or a world of the many.

But when it comes to the world of organisms, one can speak of a content of the style of productivity, and one can say that time has form. In the teleological function "from the past to the future" means the contrary: "from the future to the past". "From the past to the future" means, now, not a straight-lined flow, but a cyclic movement. This means that the style of productivity has some kind of content; and it means that the present, as unity of the opposites of past and future, has form. This form is the species of living beings. The form is the style of productivity of the historical world at this stage of organic life. This I call "subjective". Already in the biological world, past and future are confronted in the present, as the "place"; the subject forms the environment, and the environment forms the subject. The individual many are not merely that [i.e. many], but they, as single beings, are also forming themselves. Despite this, the biological world is not yet the world of absolute unity of opposites.

Only in the historical-social world of true unity of opposites are past and future simultaneously in the present, contradicting themselves. It can be said that the world, contradicting itself, is one single present. Although past and future are connected in the present, and in the teleological function of organisms, there is still a process and no true present. Therefore, there is no true production and no creation. That is why I have said that the formed is not yet separated from the forming, in the case of life in the biological sense. That is why I spoke only of a "subject". In the historical-social world, however, past and future are thoroughly confronting each other, and formed and forming are confronting each other; the formed forms even the forming, and the creature forms the creator. The single one not only passes away into the past; it also produces a producing, and this is true productivity.

The world becoming one single present means that the world becomes one single style of productivity, and that, again and again, something new or an always renewed world is born. That is the style of productivity of

179

historical creation. It is not a mere causal genesis of things, out of their environment, and no mere explicit acting of a latent [being], in the manner of a "subject" [in the organic world]. Creation is not, as Bergson thinks, a directed process which could not return to the past, even for the length of a moment; creation is essentially a genesis of thing out of the contradictory confrontation of infinite past and infinite future.

Where the straight-line is cyclic, there is creation. There is true productivity. In the historical world, that which has passed is more than something that has passed; there is, as Plato says, the non-being as being. In the historical present, past and future are facing and contradicting each other; out of this contradiction an always renewed world is born, as unity of opposites.

This I call the dialectic of historical life. If the past, as something that has already been decided, and is "given", or is taken as "thesis", than there are innumerable possibilities of ["antithesis" of] negation, and therefore there is an unlimited future. However, the past has been decided as unity of opposites, and only that which has decided the past, as unity of opposites, also decides the true future; [then] the antithesis arises necessarily, so far as the world, as unity of opposites, is creative, and as far as it is a truly living world. When the contradictory confrontation becomes deep and great, then, as unity of opposites, an always new world is created, and this is the synthesis. The creation is the more decisive, the more decisive infinite past and infinite future confront and contradict each other in the present.

180

Creation of an always new world does not only mean that the world of the past is merely negated, or gets lost; it means that the world of the past is "lifted" ("aufgehoben"), as it is called in dialectical logic. In the historical-social world, the infinite past is lifted and contained ("aufgehoben") in the present. Even after having become human beings, we have not ceased to be animal beings.

In order that past and future confront and contradict each other in the present, the present must necessarily have form. This form is the style of productivity of the historical world. Here, we see — from the individual standpoint — things through action-intuition and, here, we can say: "from the formed towards the forming". And, on the other side, where there is poiesis, and where we are acting-reflecting, there is the historical present.

The "form" of the living being is functional. Functional behaviour of living beings, means "having form". The historical present [in this case] has one single form as its style of productivity. But in the style of productivity of living beings there is, as has been said, no true confrontation of past and future and there is no true historical present. Therefore, it can not yet be said that the present, as unity of opposites, determines itself, or that the form determines itself. Therefore, the behaviour of living beings is not yet acting-reflecting; it is, in Hegel's words, still "in itself", "an sich", not "in and for itself" ("an und für sich").

With the historical-social style of productivity it is different. Here, the world is one single present in which infinite past and infinite future confront each other; here, the present, as unity of opposites, has its peculiar form, while it is, at the same time, moving endlessly; here the present determines itself, and the form determines itself.

Taking "present" merely in an abstract sense, "from present to present" must seem to be like a jump, without any mediation, but in the dialectic [of historical productivity], confrontation is already synthesis, and synthesis confrontation. There is no synthesis without confrontation, and no confrontation without synthesis. Synthesis and confrontation are two things, and still essentially one. In practical dialectic, the synthesis is not merely a need of our reason, but the "form" of reality or the "style of productivity" of the world of reality. In the world of the present, that unity of opposites, where infinite past and infinite future, absolutely negating each other, are joining, the "synthesis" is something like Hegel's "idea" ("Idee"). The synthesis does not deny confrontation; therefore, it is moving, as unity of opposites, negating itself.

The historical present as unity of the opposites of past and future, encloses the contradiction in itself, and has in itself always something "transcendent", i.e. something that has surpassed the Self. Something transcendent is always [at the same time] immanent. A transcending of the Self, and a negation of the Self, lies in the very fact that the present has form, and encloses in itself the past and the future. Such a world is essentially [self-] expressive and is a world that forms itself. This is to be understood in the same sense as the individual which, as monad, mirrors the world, and is at the same time a viewpoint of perspective.

The world, enclosing something that transcends the Self, forms itself through expression and representation. In the world where past and future, contradicting each other, are joining, we see things through acts of expression. Because we are seeing things in such a manner, it can be said that we are acting. Such acting is not mechanical and not teleological, but "logical". That which is moving by itself as unity of opposites, is [truly] "concrete", is logically "true". But in a world of straight-lined time, where there is no present, there is no "we are acting".

In looking at our self-consciousness, we understand all this much better: the unity of opposites as joining of past and future in the present, the "from the formed towards the forming", and the "from the present to the present". Our self-consciousness actually consists in the joining of past and future in the plane of present consciousness, and in the movement of this [joining], as unity of opposites. The unity of consciousness, namely the Self, is not possible in a merely straight-lined process. All the phenomena of my consciousness are many and, at the same time, — as mine — also one. This is unity of opposites in the shown sense. Even the Self of those who deny the possibility of such unity of opposites, is thinking in the way of unity of opposites. I do not say all this in order to explain the objective world through the experience of the unity of consciousness; on the contrary: our Self is of such a kind because we are

183

individuals of a world of unity of the opposites of the many and the one, because we are monadic.

It has been said above that in the historical-social world subject and environment confront each other and form each other. This means that past and future oppose each other in the present, as unity of opposites, and move from the formed towards the forming. Now, there are no such things as given data in the historical world. "Given" here means "formed". Environment, too, is essentially something formed by history. The forming of the environment by the subject, in the historical world, does not mean the forming of a material by a form. Even the material world forms itself in the way of unity of opposites. But in the world of the historical present, as unity of opposites, there are more essential ways of determining itself, and more essential kinds of productivity. They are thought as historical species; they are the different forms of society. What we call "society", is essentially a style of poiesis. Therefore, society has necessarily an ideal element; and this is the difference between the historical and the biological species. In so far as a society is intellectually productive, in so far as it is real poiesis, in a deeper sense, it is "living".

But such ideal productivity means, in my opinion, no separation from the historical-material ground. It is no mere "becoming cultural". This would mean separation of the creative subject from the environment, a fading-away of the subject, a bottomless idealisation of the idea [as a living form].

The subject forms the environment. But the environment, though formed by the subject, is more than a part of the subject; it opposes and denies it. Our life is being poisoned by that which it has produced itself, and must die. In order to survive, the subject must, again and again, begin a new life. It must, as a species of the historical world of unity of opposites, become historically productive. It must become a spiritual forming force of the historical world. Its product must have a world-wide horizon; it must make the whole world its environment. Only such a subject can live eternally.

If the subject, as historical species, acts and creates with a world-wide horizon, there is no fear that the subject would get lost, that the peculiarity of the subject would get lost, and that the subject itself would become merely general. On the contrary, it must be said that the world of unity of opposites, where infinite future and infinite past are enclosed and enveloped by the present, has one style of productivity, and that in this style of productivity different subjects are living together in one world-wide environment, each of them being for itself spiritually productive, and touching eternity.

This does not deny all subjective peculiarity, as in an abstract general world, nor does it unite all subjects teleologically in one single subject. The existence of a species as subject does not always coincide with one peculiar form of culture. Subjects which are not spiritually creative in any way, will not persist in the history of the world. The idea is essentially the principle of "life" of a subject.

Everything that, as formed, has already got the

185

character of environment, and has no more force to form the forming, is mere culture, separated from the subject. A perspective which sees the world merely as something formed, is only "cultural" [not philosophical].

2.

In the world as unity of opposites, moving from the formed towards the forming, past and future, negating each other, join in the present; the present, as unity of opposites, has form, and moves, forming itself, from present to present. The world moves, as one single present, from the formed to the forming. The form of the present, as unity of opposites, is a style of the productivity of the world. This world is a world of poiesis.

In such a world, seeing and acting are a unity of opposites. Forming is seeing, and from seeing comes acting. We see things, acting-reflecting, and we form because we see. When we speak of acting, we begin with the individual subject. But when acting, we are not outside the world, but in the world. Acting is essentially "being acted". If our acting is not merely mechanical or teleological, but truly forming, then the forming must be, at the same time, a "being formed". We are essentially forming, as individuals of a world which forms itself.

This world in which past and future, negating each other, are joining in the present, and which, as one single

186

present, moves by itself through unity of opposites, can be said to be moving through the contradictory joining of infinite past and infinite future. With this I want to say that, in one direction, the world can be thought like Leibniz' world of monads. In that world of monads, innumerable individuals are determining themselves, opposing, negating and joining each other. The monad is moving from its own center and it is a continuity of time, where the present is pregnant with the future, carrying the past on its back. The monad is a world in itself. But this relationship between the individuals and the world is, after all, nothing else but "representation = expression", as Leibniz says. The monad mirrors the world, and is, at the same time, a viewpoint of perspective.

But with regard to this world of unity of the opposites of the many and the one, the opposite can be said, namely that one single world expresses itself in innumerable ways. The world where innumerable individuals, negating each other, are united, is one single world which, negating itself, expresses itself in innumerable ways.

In this world, one thing confronts the other thing by expression, and past and future, negating each other, have joined in the present. In this world, the present encloses in itself always something that has transcended itself; here, the transcendent is immanent, and the immanent is transcendent.

Neither in the mechanical world "from the past to the future", nor in the teleological world "from the future to the past" is there any objective expression. In

187

the world of expression, the fact that the many are many, encloses the one, and the fact that the one is one, encloses the many. The present is unity of opposites; the past, although it has passed away into nothing, is still effective; and the future, although it has not yet come, shows itself already. Here (in the space of history) things are opposing each other, and acting on each other through expression; consequently they are neither causal, as necessity from the past, nor teleological, as necessity from the future. All this is valid only in the historical world which, as unity of opposites, and as one single present, moves from present to present, and is a world which forms itself from the formed towards the forming.

If it is said that the world, forming itself, moves by itself from the formed to the forming, this may appear as a jump and without mediation. It could also be questioned whether there was any room for the real acting of individuals. But my opinion is just the opposite.

Essentially and necessarily, an individual determines himself through expression, and acts through perform-ances of expression. The form the world has is essentially a contradictory connection, as unity of opposing indivi-duals. On the other hand, the acts of expression by these innumerable individuals are essentially nothing else but self-expression of the world as unity of opposites in innumerable ways.

Let us, for a moment, regard the unity of our con-sciousness, and proceed from there: Each phenomenon of consciousness is [somewhat] independent, and expresses itself. Each pretends [at the same time] to be the Self.

The Self is not like a brand mark of sheep, as James said, but that which has its form as negating unity of the self-expressing [phenomena of consciousness]. This is called our "character", or our "personality". The Self is not "outside", in a transcendent sense; our Self is there where we are conscious of ourselves. In each moment, our consciousness claims to be the whole Self. Our true Self is there where our consciousness negates and unites [the singular acts]. Past and future, negating each other, are also joining in our self-consciousness. The whole Self, as one single present of the unity of the opposites of past and future, is productive and creative. Also the "unity of consciousness" is a concrete individual of the world which forms itself through expression, although it [the unity of consciousness] is ordinarily considered abstract and separated from the world.

The world of unity of opposites, where the individual determines itself as individual through expression, is a mere "physical world", if the individual many, in negation of their own selves, are considered a mere multitude of points. The physical world is a world of mechanical laws which can be expressed in mathematical symbols. But when each individual is thought to express the world in its peculiar way, then the world is organic, and is the world of life. That which adapts itself to its environment belongs to the world of biology. There the individual does not really have "expression". But when the individual determines itself through [self-] expression, the world is historical-social, and is the world of man. Here, the world progressively forms itself as the present of

189

unity of opposites.

The material world has "form", just as the biological world. But both are not productive and are not creative. Therefore, one cannot truly say of them "from present to present", and "from the formed towards the forming". But when past and future, negating each other, join in the present, then there is no more time which flows from the past to the future, but the plane of consciousness. The historical world has the character of consciousness.

If one does not accept the function of "expression", then the movement from form to form must seem to be without mediation; function and form are regarded as independent of each other. But "acting" is [possible] only in the connection of the whole world, and only in the form of the whole world. This is also true of physical phenomena. (Lotze has shown this in his "Metaphysics"). Form and function (—form as style of productivity—) can not be thought to be independent. Usually, it is true, one imagines "function" or "activity" in an abstract way as separated from the connection of the whole of the world. Physical or biological functions may be thought in this way, but, by no means, the function of expression.

In the world as unity of opposites, where the subject forms the environment, and the environment forms the subject, the material world is also something formed, and the formed, as environment, progressively forms the subject. The evolution progresses from the material world to the biological world, and further to the world of man. In this manner, reality moves by itself, although it is impossible to think the unity of opposites within the forms

190

of abstract logic.

Our acting in this world is a forming of things; we see things through "action-intuition", and act in this way, because the individual is individual only in so far as it participates in the forming of the world, through acts of expression, and in so far as it is one side of the self-determination of the world, as unity of opposites. Action-intuition means our forming of objects, while we are formed by the objects. Action-intuition means the unity of the opposites of seeing and acting.

When past and future, negating each other, join in the present, when, therefore, the present, as unity of opposites, encloses past and future, and when the present has "form", then I say: the world forms itself. This world proceeds, as one single present, from the formed towards the forming, forming itself infinitely. We are forming, by consciously mirroring this world; we are forming the world by acts of expression. (Expression is acting through the mediation of the world). This is our "life".

Seeing things through action-intuition, means apprehending them according to the style of productivity. In this sense, the seeing of things is a mirroring of the world. Hegel's conceptual comprehension of reality must have been something of this kind. The comprehension of things according to the "concrete concept" must mean this: we, as forming and being formed, comprehend things historically according to the style of productivity. The essence of things, comprehended in this way, is the "concrete concept". The concrete concept is conceived

191

not by abstraction, but by action-intuition. Forming is here a seeing, and expression is representation.

The origin of our acting lies in the fact that we are mirroring the world. We are forming things through action-intuition, and so we comprehend reality historically, according to the style of productivity, or according to the concrete concept. Therefore, the artist's creative activity, too, is, in accordance with the style of productivity, a comprehension of the concrete concept of things, through his production. (In this sense, beauty is also truth).

The world in which infinite past and future join in the present, and which, as unity of opposites, forms itself more and more, can be expressed or represented in symbols. Experimental science comprehends in such a world-perspective the style of productivity, or, so to say, the concrete concept of things. The scientific experiment is, here, what I call action-intuition. The science of physics does not begin only with abstract logic; it begins with the world being mirrored in the Self; it begins with "representation=expression". The style of productivity of the world is, here, represented in symbols and is mathematical.

Action-intuition is no mere passive vision. A passive vision, separated from action, is perhaps thinkable, as abstract concept, but it does not exist in the world of reality. When the concrete concept is thought as style of productivity of the world which moves as unity of opposites, then it can be said that the reasonable is real, and the real is reasonable [as in Hegel]. And the word

192

"hic Rhodos, hic salta!" has its place here. The reality of action-intuition is always the place of the contradiction, and the matter is decided here. And here, too, it is decided whether the thought is true or false.

Man, mirroring the world as a Self which has acts of expression, is conscious, and, with regard to the act, "intentional". If such an act is constitutive as a mere act, then it is abstract-logical. "Act of abstraction" means: the Self which realizes acts of expression mirrors the world through symbols (through language).

But one follows the concrete logic by constructing things through acts of expression, by seeing these things in reality through action-intuition, and by so comprehending the style of productivity of the world which forms itself. Action-intuition does not mean self-representation of the whole at once, and without mediation; it means that our Self is contained in the world as an act of formation of the world.

The individual is an individual because and in so far as it forms itself through acts of expression. The individual has its Self only through self-negation, and it is [at the same time] a viewpoint of the world which forms itself. The world is progressively forming itself, and it is the negating unity of innumerable individuals which have and realize acts of expression. In so far as the individual in such a world contains self-formation of the world, it is infinitely "desiring". "Desiring" does not mean that we are merely mechanical or merely teleological; it means that we are mirroring the world in ourselves; it means that we make the world the medium for the formation

193

of the Self.

Even the life of animals is of this kind, because it is conscious. Even an animal, the higher it is developed, has already something like a "picture" of the world. Of course, not in a conscious or self-conscious manner. But the instinctive act of the animal must be something like an act of formation. It may be called "un-conscious" in the sense of E.v.Hartmann. The animal has instinct in so far as it bears within itself, unconsciously, the world which forms itself.

The world of unity of opposites is a world in which past and future, negating each other, join in the present; it is a world which, as one single present, progressively forms itself; it is, as "from the formed towards the forming", infinitely productive and creative. This world, as from the formed towards the forming, and as from the past towards the future, is at first productive in the sense of biology. The bodily life of living beings is such an act of formation. Already here the individual must be not merely mechanical or merely teleological, but "forming". This is true of the individual as far as it is conscious, though only in the bodily way of an animal. Therefore, it can be said that the behaviour of animals is impulsive and, as formation, instinctive, namely bodily. There, seeing is already acting, and acting is seing, i.e. constructive. The "body" is the system of unity of the opposites of seeing and acting. But in biological life, the formed and the forming are not truly confronted; the formed is not yet independent of the forming; therefore it can not be said that the formed forms the forming.

There it can not yet be said that the world, as one single present of unity of opposites, truly forms itself. The present is not yet form, and the world is not yet truly forming. Biological life is not creative. The individual has not yet acts of expression and it is not "free". I have said above that in the historical world, the subject forms the environment, and the environment forms the subject; biological life, however, is not subjective, but follows the environment. There is no true movement from the formed towards the forming, but only from one formed to another formed.

When I say this, it may seem to contradict my earlier statement that biological life is subjective. But in the world of biological life subject and environment have not yet become a true unity of opposites. In the world of true unity of opposites, the subject submerges in the environment, and negates itself; this means that the true Self is living. The environment encloses the subject, and forms it; this means: the environment negates itself, and so becomes subject. The forming negates itself, and becomes the formed; this means: it now becomes truly the forming. That is what I call "from the formed towards the forming".

In the world of biology, subject and environment oppose each other. The subject forms the environment; and this means, on the contrary, that it is formed by the environment. To be merely subject is the reason for being merely environment. But that subject which subsists on the environment, by submersion of the Self into the environment, is the historical subject. Here, the

195

environment is not merely given, but formed. Here, it can be said that the subject truly frees itself of the environment. The world of biological life is not yet "in and for itself".

The world of biological life, as it has been shown above, is already a unity of opposites, too, but the historical world is complete unity of opposites, as moving from the formed towards the forming, and so it is on evolution of the world of living beings to the world of man. So historical life makes itself "concrete"; the world becomes something that truly moves by itself. I do not want to say that this evolution is merely a continuity of biological life, nor that it is merely negation of biological life. It means that the historical world is through and through unity of opposites. Biological life already contained the contradiction; but biological life is still in accordance with the environment, and not yet truly "from the formed towards the forming". At the extreme limit of the contradiction, the evolution leads to the life of man. Of course, this is the result of the work of the historical life for many millions of years. At the extreme limit of acting life from the formed towards the forming, a stage is reached where the subject lives by submerging into the environment, and the environment is environment by negating itself, and becoming subjective. Past and future, contradicting each other, join in the present, and the world, as unity of opposites, progresses from present to present, forming itself; i.e. the world is productive and creative. The body is no longer a mere biological body, but a historical one. We have our body really when we are forming. Man's body is "productive".

As biological beings, we "desire", since we are mirroring the world and denying ourselves. We form instinctively. In the world of unity of opposites, from the formed towards the forming, our "desire" is a kind of forming through expression. We have the desire to produce. Therefore, we, as individuals of the world of unity of the opposites of the many and the one, are true individuals. We form the world by acts of expression. This means, on the contrary, and at the same time that we form ourselves as viewpoints of the world. The world forms itself, as negating unity of innumerable individuals which form themselves. This can rightly be asserted already of the instinctive forming of living beings. The instinct, too, must be understood as relationship between the living being and the world. (Behaviourism). The instinct of man is essentially not mere bodily forming, but a forming with the "historical body", i.e. "producing".

Man's action originates from mirroring the world through acts of expression, by seeing things productive-bodily. Seeing things through action-intuition means seeing them productive-bodily. We see things productive-bodily, and from there we act. Seeing and acting form a unity of opposites in the productive-bodily Self. Seeing things productive-bodily means comprehending them according to the style of productivity, that is as "concrete concept". It means the comprehension of things by the self-expressing Self, and from the standpoint of the present of unity of opposites. This is the standpoint of concrete logic; here is the true and the real.

197

Abstract knowledge is far from this standpoint. But without the standpoint of the experiment, there is no objective knowledge. The scientific standpoint does not deny this standpoint, but remains there, consistently. The contradiction lies in the very fact that we are acting-intuitioning and that we are productive-bodily. Therefore, we are progressing, as unity of opposites, from the formed to the forming, and we transcend the "given", as something formed. It is to be expected that we finally reach something that has transcended [even] action-intuition, [and] the body. This [transcending], however, must start from here, and return here.

The world in which past and future, negating each other, join in the present, and which, as present of the unity of opposites, forms itself, is through and through un-bodily, and is represented in symbols. It is intellectual. But this does not mean that it is completely separated from our historical body.

Everything that is given to us in the world of unity of opposites is given to us as a "task". Our task in this world is "to form". In this we have our life. We are born with this task. That which is given, is not merely to be negated, or to be mediated; it is given to be "completed". It is something bodily given. We have not been born with nothing, but with our body. It can be said that a task is put before us by the historical nature through the fact that we are born with a body. In this task is contained an infinite number of tasks (like the eye of an insect), as unity of opposites. The fact that we are born with a body, means that we are born and loaded with human tasks. That which is truly and directly given to our human acting Self confronts us objectively as an earnest task.

Reality is enveloping and conditioning us. Reality is neither merely material, nor mediating; it speaks to our Self: "Do this, or die!" The truly given is where the world, as one single present of unity of opposites, confronts me. The truly given, or true reality must be something that is to be found. We have that which is truly given to us, when we know where the contradiction of reality is. The mere "given" is nothing else but an abstract idea. We are a unity of opposites because we have a body. The world which confronts us in action-intuition demands our answer: Life or death?

The quality of our Self, as individual of the world of unity of opposites, is determined by the function of expression. We act by seeing things productive-bodily, and through action-intuition. As "from the formed towards the forming", we have our body in and with the formed; i.e. we are historical-bodily. But this means that we human beings are social beings. The "homo faber" is "zōon politikon" and, therefore, "logon echōn".

The basis of the social structure is the family; it is the origin of human society. According to the theory of descendence, the family, too, would be to be reduced to the group-instinct of animals. The gorilla lives with many females, similar to some primitive men. But in the instinctive grouping of animals, and in human society, instinct and culture are essentially different, as Malinowski and others say. (Malinowski "Sex and Repression in

199

Savage Society"). Already something like the "Oedipus Complex" shows that the human family is social, and different from the animal group.

As primitive as a human society might be, it still contains individuality. Despite its group-character, it contains also the behaviour of individuals, which is essentially not group-behaviour. Therefore, human society is essentially something that progresses, being formed, and forming, while the animal group, founded on instinct, is something [merely] "given". While most scholars regard primitive society as a mere group-structure, I agree with Malinowski who asserts that savage society contains, from the beginning, the "person". Even in savage society, the concept of "sin" can be found. (Malinowski: "Crime and Customs in Savage Society"). This shows that society in contrast to the group which is based on instinct, is moving as unity of the opposites of the many and the one, and from the formed towards the forming.

The human individual acts essentially not instinctively through adaptation, but forming through expression. Society begins with supression of instincts, and, therefore, incest, for instance, [or its repression] plays an important role in primitive society. Where the relationship between man and wife, between parents and children, and between brothers and sisters is "fixed" not by instinct, but by insinuation, we speak of "society". Where lies the basis of the origin of society?

As I have already said, it lies in that which is "from the formed towards the forming", which is to say, in the unity of the opposites of subject and environment. It can be said that society begins with "poiesis". Several characteristics could be given for the difference between primitive society and the instinctive animal group; but they all must begin with poiesis. This is the reason why I regard society as historical-bodily. Society can also be thought as an economic mechanism, because it is necessarily through and through material-productive. There it has its real basis. But it is, naturally, poiesis. Man differs from animal in that he has tools. The economic mechanism of society develops from the formed towards the forming. The family-system can also be looked at from the side of its economic mechanism. With regard to the origin of property, the opinions of the scholars are divided; but so much is evident: property comes from our historical-bodily nature, because we have our body in and with things.

Seen from another side, the world, forming itself as unity of opposites, is "from the environment to the subject". I have said that this was peculiar to organic life, but that does not mean that man had already left it behind. When it comes to the world of man, as unity of opposites, there is a transition from mere instinct to a forming through expression. This means that the environment, through self-negation, becomes subjective.

In the world of man, as unity of opposites, the subject is essentially subject by submerging in the environment, and the environment is essentially environment by becoming subjective through self-negation. This quality of the world is identical with the fact that the individual,

201

acting through expression, and mirroring the world in itself, is essentially one side and one perspective of the world which forms itself; and as such, the individual has its subject in the objective world. Having our Self in things, means having property. Having property, is not merely rooted in the action of the individual, but must be recognized by the objective world. Property must find its expression in the [objective] world, as belonging to a certain individual; it must be recognized by the [objective] sovereignty. The world which, as unity of the opposites of the many and the one, forms itself through expression, is necessarily related to "law". Our having the body in and with things, is necessarily related to law.

Also according to Hegel ("Philosophy of Law §29), it is through the law that [our] existence is regarded as immersed in free will. The fact that we, moving from the formed towards the forming, have "poiesis", and are historical-bodily, means that our society is not instinctive, but lawful. "Poiesis" is possible only in a world which also has legal significance.

According to the sociologists, the production of primitive society, too, has a legal order in a wider sense. These social systems can also, from another point of view, be called forms of possible development of productive poiesis; they are different kinds of the historical style of productivity. The world of historical productivity is, as movement from the formed towards the forming, essentially productive and creative in a material sense, as far as its character as environment is concerned. Here lies the basis of Machiavelli's "raison d'état", and here lie the conditions for the possibility of a historical-productive world.

The world, forming itself, and progressing from the formed towards the forming, is necessarily material-productive, as it is "from the formed". Society must have an economic mechanism, it is a material style of production. But this does not mean that the world is mechanical, nor that it is merely teleological, but that the world forms itself, as one single present. There the historical act of formation must have already been effective, as unity of opposites.

The world, as unity of opposites, necessarily touches the absolute. In the basis of the origin of society, something "religious" is active. Therefore, primitive society is mythical. Myth is a living reality, dominating in primitive human society. (Malinowski "Myth in Primitive Psychology"). It is said that the old religions were more social systems than religions. (Robert Smith). I believe that something Dionysian [Nietzsche "das Dionysische"] is active at the root of the origin of society. I am inclined to agree with Harrison that the gods were born out of the Dionysian dance. (Harrison, "Themis"). It is said that a certain civilisation originates when a certain people lives in a certain geographical environment. Of course, the geographical environment forms an important factor in the formation of a civilisation. But the geographical environment does not form culture [as such]. Of the people, too, it can not be said that it was there, in a latent form, before its historical form came into being. A people is being formed by its own forming.

When the world, as one single present which is a unity of opposites, forms itself, then it is a world of life, a world of infinite forms. The form of life of animals is instinctive, that of man is "demonic".[1] And just as with animals, it is a truly living species, in so far as it is, as a movement, from the formed towards the forming, creative.

The people is just such a demonic force of formation. "From the formed towards the forming" means here: that which is formed by the species, forms the forming. So it is intellectual and universal ["universal" in the sense of universal history]. The forming of the species is one kind of historical productivity. To progress in this direction, as unity of opposites, is historical evolution.

Like the instinctive behaviour of animals, our acting begins with our mirroring of the world, in the way of unity of opposites. We are historical-bodily. This means that our acting originates in society. Also the personal opposites of "I" and "you" come from social evolution. The self-consciousness of the child develops out of social relations. The reason is that society originates as a self-forming of the one present which is unity of opposites.

Just as there is a body in biological life, as formation in the way of unity of opposites — and that is what we usually call "body", — so there is a historical body in historical life acting-reflecting,— and that is what we usually call "society". Acting-reflecting, or action-intuition means: we, as individuals of the world which,

---

1) This idea of "demonic" is related to Goethe's "das Dämonische".

as unity of opposites, forms itself, comprehend this world according to its style of productivity. It means: we comprehend the world, according to Hegel, by concept. It means: we grasp reality through poiesis.

This acting-reflecting, historical-bodily society is based on unity of opposites, and is progressing in contradictions, transcending itself. This progressing by transcending itself, however, involves no separation from the real basis. Such separation would lead to a merely abstract world. But the world of action-intuition should not be denied from the standpoint of abstract logic. The negation must arise from contradictions in reality itself.

That which is "given", is given historically and individually. The contradiction of life lies in the concept of life itself. And the contradiction always remains [in progressing evolution]. In human life, the contradiction reaches its maximum. Seen from the point of view of the contradiction, there is no possibility of avoiding it. That is the reason why religious men speak of original sin. As descendents of Adam, we are all born with the hereditary sin.

3.

The world which, as the present of unity of opposites, forms itself, is a world of unity of the opposites of the many and the one; and we, as individuals of such a world, and determining ourselves, are essentially "desiring", we are essentially "will to live". But the world has born us, and will kill us. The world confronts us with unceasing pressure, threatening us. We are living while struggling with the world.

Something like a mere "given" may be thought with regard to the abstract intellectual Self; but that which is given us as individuals, is put before us as a "life or death?" task—(so the world asks us). The world which is given to the individual Self, is not a general world, but a singular one. The more we are individuals, the more this is true. This can also be expressed in the opposite way: the more the world is singular, the more individual is the individual. Therefore, it can be said that the individual is an individual by confronting the absolute unity of opposites, or "the absolute". The individual is an individual by making its own life and its own death a means of mediation. It makes "action-intuition" a means of mediation. Here is also the reason for the appearance of the species of living beings. The individual is always confronted with the absolute unity of opposites; it is confronted with that which asks: "life or death?" Because here, through unity of opposites, one common style of productivity originates, the individual lives. And there are different species, because different styles of productivity are possible. In the world of unity of the opposites of the many and the one, a species originates when and in so far as the contradiction is resolved ("aufgehoben"). The life of the species originates when and in so far as there is action-intuition. Life as well as species is already dialectical.

One can speak of the "life" of the species in so far

as the species lives in and through the individuals, and the individuals live in and through the species. Life is always a moving by itself, and as far as there is a moving by itself there is life. Dialectical evolution is not to be regarded as a negation of the given, from outside; it is essentially this: the given itself, contradicting itself, progresses by transcending its own self from within. Already life in the biological sense, is neither mechanical nor teleological, and that which is fixed today as "species" is but the result of an infinite dialectical evolution, and will change at some time and disappear. Although one commonly speaks of a fixed species, each species changes within certain limits. Fixation of the species means only that the species has reached a certain typical and normative form.

It may be surprising to use the words "action-intuition" and "concept" with regard to animals, but the life of animals too is, as self-determination of the self-contradicting, one single present, capable of formation; [already here], seeing and acting are inseparable. The animal eye, for example, is the result of a formation in the way of unity of opposites; it can not be separated from the life of the species.

Where reality is grasped in the way of unity of opposites, there is action-intuition. It means that the creative style of productivity is grasped. In biological life, too, the species originated through such a dialectical process. Therefore, an "idea" can be thought within the basis of the species. This idea is not "ideal" or "intellectual", but — as in the philosophy of Hegel — an

207

act of dialectical formation. Intuition, separated from action, is either merely an abstract idea, or mere illusion.

Life is an infinite moving by itself. There are always infinite directions, and infinite possibilities of [imaginary] illusion. The more life is of the kind of "unity of opposites", the more is this true. The deeper we are in individuality, the richer is the illusion. So, when in the way of unity of opposites, a forming is realized, where we are acting-reflecting, there is our individual life, there is our true Self. There we are confronted with that which asks us: "life or death?"

If our action separates itself from this action-intuition, it becomes merely mechanical or teleological. Even moral obligation, if separated from practical realisation, is merely formal. The life of our species, too, is the result of an infinite dialectical evolution. But if we would act only according to the tradition, only in the way of the species, it would mean a mechanisation of the Self, and the death of the species. We must be creative, from hour to hour.

Action-intuition does not mean that the whole presents itself, at once, in a passive manner. In such a case, the Self would get lost, it would become a mere universal or general. On the contrary, action-intuition means that we as individuals confront in the way of unity of opposites, the world, which confronts and opposes us, i.e. that we become creative. By saying that the individual always confronts the absolute unity of opposites, i.e. that which asks "life or death?", I mean that it is life and death which make the individual an individual. The individual lives and dies; otherwise it would not be an individual. Biological life, too, is life and death of the single living being. Death is an entering into absolute nothingness; life is an appearing out of absolute nothingness.

All this is true only for the self-determination of the present, identical in contradiction. Biological life, too, is essentially forming; there is already something like action-intuition.

Productivity through action-intuition means: the individual confronts transcendence, confronts the absolute, and has as mediation the unity of opposites. From this standpoint of the individual appears true moral obligation, the "ought". Otherwise it [the individual] becomes arbitrary. The concrete obligation originates necessarily from our own self-contradiction. We live our most individual existence through that which denies us. Already as desiring bodily existence, we have an existence which negates itself. True moral obligation confronts us from without as stipulation of transcendence. It comes into appearance through true poiesis. (Action-intuition always serves as medium for true poiesis). In the depth of our existence we are in contradiction with ourselves, because we are bodily. And since we are historical-bodily, we have, through and through, ought-character. The concrete obligation does not come from mere logical contradiction. That which confronts us as the true absolute is not a logically thought absolute; it is that which in reality asks us: "life or death?"

The world as unity of opposites, from the formed towards the forming, essentially forms itself as one present, identical in contradiction, and progresses in this way. The world, moving from the formed to the forming, has as its center an acting-reflecting present, and contains a plane of consciousness, where its own self is infinitely mirrored.

If endless past and endless future join, in contradiction, in the present, then there must be a standpoint where time is extinguished. The self-formation of the present, identical in contradiction, has essentially consciousness as its element. The activity of forming is neither mechanical, nor merely teleological, but essentially "conscious". If one says that the world, as one single present of unity of opposites, forms itself, it means, at the same time, that the present transcends the present, and that consciousness, by mirroring something that has transcended itself, is "intentional". The world which has as its center the present, identical in contradiction, is necessarily expressed by symbols. Even from the standpoint of acting-reflecting reality, it is possible to think the world through expression [in symbols], to think of the world abstractly through concepts. This self-negation is one element of the world as unity of opposites.

We are always confronted with absolute unity of opposites, and the more we are individuals, the more is this true. This is the reason why it can be said that the world which progresses, forming itself as unity of opposites, is through and through "logical". In self-formation of the present, as unity of opposites, the world is "moving", while time is extinguished on the plane of consciousness. Even action-intuition can be ignored. It can be thought that we think and act freely. We separate ourselves from that which confronts us as unity of opposites. There is a world of abstract freedom.

This, however, is a direction in which we, in reality, lose the world, and lose ourselves. On the contrary, our consciousness appears as one moment of self-formation of the world of absolute unity of opposites. And vice versa: the contradictory joining of past and future in the present in our consciousness, means essentially that the world, contradicting itself, forms itself. To the degree in which we are consciously free, we are in a contradictory sense confronted with the absolute unity of opposites. By being individuals of the world which, as present of unity of opposites, forms itself, we are through and through confronted with that which asks us: "life or death?" That is the reason why our acts of consciousness have a normative character.

As I have already said, action-intuition, as I call it, is neither instinctive nor artistic. Of course, it can be said that instinct is its not yet developed form, and that art is an extreme border-case. But, [essentially], action-intuition is the fundamental and most concrete form of conscious comprehension of reality. The "concept" is not formed by "abstraction". To comprehend something by concept, means to comprehend it through action-intuition. Through action-intuition we conceive a thing conceptually '('gainen" is "Begriff"[1]).

---

1) Nishida uses the German word, "Begriff", concept; "gainen" is the Japanese word which also means "concept".

Conceiving and grasping something through action-intuition, means: seeing it through formation, comprehending it through poiesis. I have said that we are forming the things, and that, on the other hand, at the same time, the things, while formed by us, are forming us by themselves, as something independent; and I have said that we are born out of the world of things. All this means that we grasp reality through action-intuition, while the act, from the formed towards the forming, is contained in the object, contradicting itself. Such conceptual knowledge is possible only in a world which forms itself, as [one] present of unity of opposites. The self-forming of the world as present of unity of opposites, has the character of consciousness, as has been said above. As forming factors of such a world, we grasp reality through action-intuition, i.e. through poiesis. This is the essence of our conceptual knowledge. What we, today, call conceptual knowledge, is essentially that which we have gained through action-intuition, by forming things. We have gained it through poiesis.

In general, it is the eye which is regarded as having the character of pure knowledge, and as being theoretical, independent from practical application. But, just as Aristotle said that we are intelligent because we have hands, so I believe that conceptual knowledge has been gained "from our hands". Our hand is an instrument,— an instrument to grasp, as well as an instrument to produce. (Noiré "Das Werkzeng")

At the transition from animal to man, we become social beings. In society there are already individuals.

Society originates in poiesis as centre. Our conceptual knowledge must have originally developed from social production. The concept of "thing" must have originally been conceived through social production. The origin of conceptual knowledge lies, I think, in the style of production[1] of [self-forming] things which have been conceived through social production.

Without language there is no thinking, and language, as the philologists say, accompanied originally a common social activity [and production]. Conceptual knowledge is true in so far as it is productive according to the style of its productivity. Modern science, too, has developed from this standpoint, and cannot be separated from it. Although modern science has already transcended this standpoint, and even denies it, science started there, and it returns there. Modern science has essentially technical significance.

Experiment, although it has the character of pure knowledge, is essentially a grasping of reality through action-intuition. Of course, science and experiment are not one and the same; but experiment and theory can not be separated in science. The theory, as theoretical as it may be, has essentially developed from acting-reflecting comprehension of the style of productivity of things, through poiesis. Historically, all theory develops from there. Without the basis of action-intuition, there is no science. In this sense, Minkowski says in his lectures

---

1) "Style of production" has here the significance of the principle of self-formation of things (This footnote is added by the translater).

213

about the relativity of space and time, that this theory was born out of physical experiments, and that its strength lies therein.

When we say that the world, as present of the unity of the opposites of past and future, forms itself, we are confronted with that which asks us: "life or death?", in short, we confront the one world. The more we are individuals, the more is this true. And it can be said: the more we are individuals, the more we are, on the contrary, one with the world, in the way of unity of opposites.

In so far as the world has the character of a plane of consciousness, and we the character of acts of consciousness, the world can be called a "logical universal". The "act of judgement" means: comprehending things, acting-reflecting, as an individual Self. Knowledge of objective reality through judgements is there where we, as individual selves in the present, at the point of the individual Self, comprehend things, acting-reflecting. But what does "individual Self in the present" mean? It means: Individual in the world of unity of opposites, where past and future are one through contradiction. It means: Individual of the historical space of the absolute present. Comprehending things, acting-reflecting as such an individual Self, through poiesis, means seeing things in the historical space as absolute present. It means: the law of things becomes clear and distinct in the present which encloses past and future. It means grasping the style of productivity of the world. Here is the world of objective knowledge. It can be said that knowledge is objective in the degree in which the acting-reflecting Self is through and through individual, in the degree in which the present is absolutely present. The physicist's experimenting, for instance, is the process in which he, as an individual Self of the physical world, comprehends things through action-intuition. The world of physics, too, is not outside the historical world, but only one side of it. Here, the present of unity of opposites has no form, and the style of productivity of the world repeats itself. The style of productivity is not creative. Seen under this aspect, the historical world is "physical". The historical world, seen from one side, is necessarily also of this kind. We, too, as bodies, are materially in this world. From the beginning of historical life, socially-productive, we also see the world physically.

Modern physical science, too, has necessarily developed from there. The fact that we, as individual Selves, confront the world, means, on the other hand, that the one single world confronts us. Here exists the individual Self of the modern physicist, and here modern physical knowledge is realized through action-intuition.

The world which, uniting past and future, forms itself as absolute unity of opposites, i.e. as the absolute present, this world is through and through logical. The so-called "logical form" is merely the abstract form of self-formation of this world. On the plane of consciousness of the present of unity of opposites, the world is in movement. By transcending causal connection, we are

215

thinking and free. Judgements are possible when the acting-reflecting reality forms the "hypokeimenon". The more we are individuals, the more is this true. The world is expressed in different ways. From the standpoint of the individual the whole world is expressed, just like the monad mirrors the world. When this expression of the world, the judgement, is proved through action-intuition, i.e. by poiesis, it is "true". "Truth" is where we, as forming factors of the self-forming world, comprehend things through action-intuition.

On the other hand, it can be said that here the world proves itself. The more individual we are, as factors of the world, the more we confront and contradict the one world which as unity of opposites, forms itself in contradictions. Knowledge must follow formal logic as it is formation on the plane of consciousness where the present of unity of opposites denies time. The world is [only] in this respect in accordance with formal logic. The world is in accordance with formal logic when action-intuition is ignored, which, however, is the core of the world, forming itself as the present of unity of opposites. Formal logic does not stand outside the historical act of formation, but is contained therein. Knowledge is no mediation of logic and sensual perception, but self-determination of the concrete universal.

The self-formation of the world as present of unity of opposites, is logical; this means: as far as it is formation on the plane of consciousness, it is the concrete universal. The mirroring of the world by the monad may be seen as a perspective of the world. Objective knowledge is realized from the formed towards the forming, by grasping reality through poiesis and action-intuition, as self-determination of the universal which has the character of unity of the opposites of the many and the one, i.e. the "dialectical Universal". The true concrete universal encloses the individual, and has the character of "place". The process of action-intuition, as self-determination of the concrete universal, is essentially the process of concrete logic. Through this process inductive knowledge and scientific knowledge are effected.

As has been said above, all our actions originate as action-intuition; they originate through a mirroring of the world by individuals. (They have, therefore, the character of acts of expression). Our knowledge, too, is through and through historical action. However abstract-logical an act of knowledge may be thought, in so far as it has the value of objective knowledge, it never leaves the standpoint of grasping things through poiesis and action-intuition. However, it must, as self-determination of the present of unity of opposites, have its own logical mediation [in the historical world]. The more individual we are, and the more objective our knowledge is, the more is this true.

The conventional theory of knowledge (epistemology?) does not take the act of understanding as an act of historical formation in the historical world, i.e. within the whole process [of the self-forming world]. The act of understanding is not taken in the whole process, but as a single act of consciousness, so-to-say on a vertical line crossing history. But if it is cut, in such a way, by the plane of consciousness, and regarded as such, one sees only logic and [sensual] intuition opposing and mediating each other. Seen in the whole process, however, knowledge means essentially this: that we, as poiesis, as the historical-productive Self, are progressively grasping and apprehending reality through action-intuition. The problem does not arise abstract-logically, but out of the depth of historical life.

This does not mean that I regard truth pragmatically, however. Historical life, as self-formation of the present of unity of opposites, is intellectual [literally: "idea-teki", i.e. "idea-like"].

Action-intuition does not mean an immediate transition from passive sensual intuition to another kind of intuition, without mediation through the logic of judgement. In the world of the present of unity of opposites, individual and world are opposing each other; there is necessarily a confrontation of the formed and the forming. Seen in this way, intuition and action are opposing each other. But the relationship between both is not merely this opposition and negation, as it is seen from the point of view of the subject. There are absolute past and absolute future opposing each other. An infinite historical past oppresses us infinitely in the absolute present. Infinite past, confronting us in the present, means that the past has the quality of expression. Ordinarily it is regarded as mere object of understanding. But the fact that the past opposes us through expression, and induces us to acts of expression, means that things are presenting themselves in our intuition.

That which induces and moves the existence of our very Self, is seen intuitively, as I have said above. It has been said that in the world, which as unity of opposites moves from the formed to the forming, the environment is truly environment when it becomes subjective, contradicting itself; so now, the world in which the Self is contained, contradicting itself, is [given] by intuition; it is a world where the act, contradicting itself, is contained in the object; it is a world where action results from seeing; it is a world in which we are quasi absorbed.

In the world of absolute unity of opposites there is no mere opposing of subject and object, nor any mere mutual mediation; it is a struggle of life and death. That which is given us by intuition in the world of unity of opposites, denies not only our existence, but our soul. That which denies and kills only from outside, is not yet truly "given" in the way of absolute unity of opposites; the truly "given" leaves us alive, but enslaves and kills our soul. Fundamentally, the act, contradicting itself, is contained in the object. And the fact that the environment, contradicting itself, becomes subjective, means that it becomes [a subject, it becomes] Mephisto. Satan is hidden in the depth of the world, given by intuition. The more individual our Self is, the more is this true.

That which is given intuitively is, according to the usual opinion, passively received, and the act disappears; but this is an undialectical aspect from the point of view of the individual ego. The true aspect is where [our own]

219

action is against us. Therefore, the world of intuition is the more painful, the more individual we are.

In the world of animal instinct, too, the individual is desiring in so far as it mirrors the world; it acts from seeing. But there the individual is not truly individual. Therefore, there is also no [true] intuition. The instinctive behaviour of animals is never endangered by Satan. Intuition is something that induces our action, and spurns our Self in its depth. Still it is [usually] regarded as being a kind of image of perception, or a dream-image.

When the world, as present of unity of opposites, forms itself, then the past is past but is still there in the present, in contradiction with itself; it is nonbeing and being, at the same time. The world confronts us who are at the same time formed and forming, in the way of expression. The environment, confronting us, is [also] through and through expression. And when the environment, from the formed towards the forming, oppresses us, it is for us "intuition". It is intuition in so far as it moves the acting existence of our individual Self.

Past is past, only by negating itself, and entering into future. Past is possible because there is future, and vice versa. In history there is nothing which has been merely given; what is given, is always something formed; and it is formed in such a way that it should deny itself from the formed towards the forming. We, as forming in a world which moves from the formed towards the forming, that is to say as forming factors of the world which forms itself, we are always confronted with this world. And

220

we proceed, forming the world from the formed towards the forming; this is the standpoint of action-intuition, as I call it.

The more individual we are, as forming factors of the creative world which forms itself, as the present of unity of opposites, i.e. the more we are concrete-personal, the more we stand at the point of historical creation, acting-reflecting. In this sense it can be said that action and intuition are opposing each other. The world oppresses us through expression; this means: it penetrates deep into our Self, and demands the abdication of our soul. We are forming; this means: as individuals of a world of unity of opposites, we comprehend the world in a creative manner. The historical-creative act grasps reality; this means: concrete reason. But herein, the mediation of the logic of judgement is contained. "Reason" means: to deepen oneself, from the standpoint of action-intuition. It means: to grasp reality according to its style of productivity. The "concrete concept" (or "concrete notion") is the style of productivity or reality.

This is also the basis for scientific knowledge. The world is apprehended by a creative act; this means: it is apprehended intellectually. The "idea" is essentially the act of creation of the world. Hegel's "Idée" must be of this kind.

With poiesis as its core, at the point of its creation, the historical world is confronted with infinite past and infinite future. This confrontation and opposition in the present of unity of opposites, may be called the confrontation and opposition of subject and environment.

This opposition and forming of each other by subject and environment is neither mechanical nor teleological. The environment has the quality of expression, and in the way of intuition it penetrates the subject, the forming. Intuition means: that things want to deprive us of our Self. It does not mean an uninterested confrontation of thing and Self. Producing things, does not mean that our Self has been carried away by these things, nor that the Self has become a thing and is lost as Self. On the other hand, it also does not mean that only the Self is active. Forming means essentially a truly active grasping of the truth of things. If action-intuition meant only this, that the Self were carried away, it would not recognize logic. In action-intuition, the Self is completely active. Action-intuition does not mean an accepting of things as they are, but an active grasping. We, as forming factors of the world of unity of opposites, must necessarily be logical in this world. Negation of logic would mean an obscuring of the Self. But through action-intuition and poiesis, our Self becomes more and more distinct and clear. Art is regarded as being alogical. Artistic intuition may, in a sense, be called alogical, since it originates in that direction of action-intuition where the Self is carried away by things. In concrete logic, however, artistic intuition is contained as one direction. (Art, too, is essentially "reasonable").

From the standpoint of production, past and future oppose each other, but this is no mere opposition and confrontation, but a creative movement in the way of unity of opposites, from the formed towards the forming. Therefore, the world, as the present of unity of opposites, is forming itself, i.e. it has the character of consciousness. As unity of opposites, from the past towards the future, the world has the character of consciousness. As absolute past, the world approaches us, pressing and forcing us. But as past of a world of unity of opposites, the world presses us not merely through causation. Mere causal necessity does not deny our soul; it must be a kind of necessity which penetrates into the depth of our personal Self, as "historical past". It must be a necessity which moves us from the depth of our soul. That which confronts us in intuition as historical past from the standpoint of action-intuition, denies our personal Self, from the depth of our life. This is what is truly given to us. That which is given to our personal Self in action-intuition, is neither merely material, nor does it merely deny us; it must be something that penetrates us demonically.[1] It is something that spurns us with abstract logic, and deceives us under the mask of truth.

In opposition to this absolute past, pressing our personal Self in its depth, we ourselves take the standpoint of absolute future. We are acting-reflecting, and thoroughly forming. We are thoroughly creative, as forming factors of the creative world which forms itself. (We always have our Self in transcendence, as is said at the end of this essay). Here is the basis of idealism.

---

1) Nishida is thinking here of Goethe's concept of the demonic ("Das Dämonische").

223

Seeing the world through action-intuition implies forming the world through action-intuition.

Past is past by disappearing into the future, in contradiction to itself. Future is future by becoming past, in contradiction to itself. The world, as mere past, deprives us of our personal Self and our roots of life; this means: the world negates itself; and becomes uncreative. Intuition itself is the contradiction. In so far as the world is living, creative, and productive, it necessarily comes to contradict itself. Our acting Self grows out of the depth of this self-contradiction of the world. The manner in which the world, as absolute past, invades our personal Self through intuition, is neither mechanical nor teleological; it is a pressure that tries to compel our soul to abdicate and resign. It is not the pressure of the world as object of understanding, but as object of belief. It is something that induces us to act. This world has essentially an intellectual or spiritual character. Otherwise it would not have the power to move our personal Self, and it would not be "given" to our acting Self.

That which, as something formed, moves us in the present of unity of opposites, oppresses us with abstract logic. (It demands: since it has been like this, thou shalt act like this!)

From the standpoint of abstract logic, the world is regarded as something that has already been decided. Our Self is abstract-logical where it meets itself from the direction of the past. That is called "reflection". But concrete logic is where our acting Self, as forming factor

of the world of unity of opposites, progressively grasps
the style of productivity of the historical world through
action-intuition and poiesis.

Where there is no past there is no future. Therefore,
the past is an absolute condition for our acting. But
our action is abstract-logical when it sees everything only
from the direction of that [past] which has already been
decided. The fact that the world of unity of opposites
confronts us through action and intuition, implies that it
oppresses us with abstract logic. This pressure is realized
only in that the world, as past, provokes forming acts in
the present of unity of opposites. Concrete logic is self-
formation of the present of unity of opposites, and, as
such, has abstract logic as mediation. Abstract logic
has significance as logic only as such mediation for
concrete logic. Otherwise it [abstract logic] would be
merely a barren possibility.

By saying that we grasp reality through action-
intuition, I do not want to say that we should not have
abstract logic as mediation. On the contrary! The
more we, as forming factors of the world of unity of
opposites, are individual and creative, the more must we
be moved logically by that which is given in the present
of unity of opposites, in the form of action-intuition.
The very fact that the world forms itself in the way of
unity of opposites, is nothing else but concrete logic. In
this sense, art is also concrete-logical. I see art from the
point of view of historical human formation, and not
the other way round: historical production from the
point of view of art.

225

4.

It seems to contradict our usual way of thinking when I say: that which is given to us intuitively, moves us logically. It may sound oversophisticated. But the conventional notions of "intuition" and "the given" [data] have their origin in the intellectual Self, and not in the concrete historical-social Self. They are not seen from the standpoint of the acting and producing Self.

It is true that from the standpoint of logic of judgement, everything that is given can be regarded as being irrational, and [that, therefore,] every intuition can be regarded as being a-logical. But we, as concrete human beings, are born in the historical-social world, as acting-reflecting beings. And so far as we may proceed, we cannot abandon this standpoint. That which is given, is given historical-socially, and that which is seen by intuition, is seen acting and producing; it moves us through expression. As given in the world of unity of opposites, it penetrates into our personal Self.

Society originates as self-formation of the world of unity of opposites. However primitive a society may be, it is never merely instinctive, nor merely collective. It is essentially unity of the opposites of the one and the many. We, as personal Self, are confronted with that which is absolute unity of opposites, i.e. with transcendence. Even savage society contains individuality, as Malinowski says. Here is something fundamentally different from the herdlike grouping of animals. Primitive society is completely bound by totem and tabu, but still there is a certain freedom of the individual, because there is something like crime and sin.

That which is given to us as concrete human beings, cannot be the so-called psychological intuition [or representation]; it must be something that is given socially, something that envelopes us. As self-formation of the world of unity of opposites, it is given us as a menace; it is given us as self-determination of the dialectical Universal, as I call it. It confronts us as something social and conventional, as a postulate of the past.

Seen from the logical standpoint, we are singular [not universal]; still, as being historical-social, we are essentially moved by the species to which we belong. One may call it "pre-logical", as Lévy-Bruhl does. But even Plato's logic has as its basis the "participation with the idea". Merely abstract logic is no true logic at all. Concrete logic must be unity of the opposites of both sides. Of course, the mythical element must disappear, when logic should become true logic. Society developes dialectically from the formed towards the forming; but however far this evolution may go,— society, as a fundamentally historical-social formation, can never be separated from the historical process of action-intuition, i.e., from progressively grasping reality through poiesis. This is true with regard to concrete logic.

I do not say that in the depth of logic there is an intuitive-mystical element; I only mean that one must, by all means, approach reality by poiesis and practical

227

action. I mean that one must grasp the style of productivity of the world which forms itself as unity of
opposites. This means a progressive negation of all that
which conditions us mythically. That which is merely
singular, and merely historical, must progressively be
transcended. That which is given intuitively, is denied,
but this is not identical with the standpoint of abstract
rationalism, according to which all that is historical, is
denied, or all that is singular, is merely the singular of
the universal. Even primitive society originates essentially as unity of opposites, and our society has its evolution only from this standpoint [of unity of opposites].
Just because it represents a unity of opposites, it unfolds
itself progressively from the formed towards the forming.

That which is given historically, oppresses us in the
present of unity of opposites, as given by universal history;
it penetrates into our Self to the depth of life so that
we can deny it the less, the more we are each an
individual Self. And that which oppresses us in intuition, becomes something that presses against us with all
the weight of universal history.

The singularity of society is not mere [logical]
singularity; it is a style of productivity of the historical
world. The general opinion is that we, as individual
Self, are reasonable by abandoning all [sensual] intuition;
but it would be true to say that we are reasonable by
being active and productive as forming factors of the
world of unity of opposites.

As in primitive society, we, too, are always confronted
with the absolute unity of opposites. This is the more so,

228

the more individual we are. We become an individual Self through the very fact that we, as forming factors of the world of unity of opposites, are confronted with the absolute unity of opposites. It can even be said that only there do we become an individual Self. And we reach this point through self-formation of the world of unity of opposites, that is, concrete-logically. Concrete logic has abstract logic as mediation, but abstract logic does not open the way to concrete logic.

Hegel justifies private property by the ideal nature of the personality. The concrete personality [however] is essentially "historical-bodily". Society originates essentially as historical production from the formed towards the forming. Our Self exists as forming factor of the society which forms itself through unity of opposites. Personality must be considered from this standpoint. Human society differs from the animal group, in that there are individuals from the beginning, and in that the personal element is realized when in the unity of opposites, the individual many are confronted with the whole one. The contradictory confrontation of the many individuals with the one whole, — in the world of unity of opposites —, means on the other hand the contradictory unification of the many in the one. This means: we are personality, by being confronted with God. It, therefore, means also: by having God as mediator, I am confronted with you, one personality is confronted with another personality.

Society, as self-formation of the present of unity of opposites, moves from the formed towards the forming.

229

This process is neither mechanical nor teleological, but in the manner of action-intuition, as unity of the opposites of the many and the one. The many being the many of the one, the one being the one of the many, motion being tranquillity, and tranquillity being motion,— there must be contained the moment of self-forming of the eternal, i.e. of a spiritual ["idea-like"] formation. This is the origin of civilisation. Therefore, as self-formation of the present of unity of opposites, civilisation or culture is at the same time formation of and by the species, and is also universal. Society, which forms itself in the manner of unity of opposites, now, as spiritual formation, becomes the "state", i.e. reasonable. We become each a concrete personality, as forming factor of this society.

In this sense, it can be said that the state is logical substance[1], and that our moral actions have the state as mediation. Without civilisation, no state. An uncivilized society does not deserve the name "state". Since culture, as something spiritual, is universal, it is the forming of society by the species; but it is not always merely that.

The historical world, from the origin of living beings to man, is unity of the opposites of the many and the one. And it moves from the formed towards the forming. In the case of animal life, the individual many are not yet confronted with the one whole; the individual is not yet independent. There, the process of evolution from the formed towards the forming, is to be thought of merely

---

1) Misprint in the original Japanese text; it should be "moral substance".

as a process of the whole one, which is to say, it is teleological. The fact that the individual is not yet independent, means that the one is not yet the true one, that it is
not yet transcendent and opposing the world of the individual many. As yet it is merely the one of the many.
But in the world of man, primitive as it may still be, there
is a [true] unity of the opposites of the many and the one.

In primitive society, however, the individual is not
yet truly independent; the whole one is oppressive, it is
merely transcendent. As yet the many are merely the
many of the one. But an individual is only a real individual when it is independent.

In the world of unity of opposites it is identical to
say that the individual forms itself, and that the world
forms itself. And, the other way round, it is identical to
say that the world forms itself, and that the individual
forms itself. The many and the one, negating each
other, become that which is "from the formed towards
the forming".

Such an element must be contained in the world of
unity of opposites, and this very element is the process
of civilisation or culture. To let the individual many live,
is the life of the one whole, seen from this standpoint.
And the life of the whole one is the life of the individual
many. Society, as substantial freedom, becomes the moral
substance, and our action, as forming act of the historical
world, has moral significance.

Where the world of unity of opposites progressively
forms itself spiritually in the way of unity of opposites,
where we are creative through action-intuition, there is

true morality.   In this sense, the process of civilisation is essentially a moral one.   It can be said that the evolution of civilisation has as its mediation, the state as substantial freedom.   When we, as individuals of a society which represents the moral substance, are creative, our actions are moral actions; the society is the moral substance in so far as it is spiritually formative, as a forming act of the world of unity of opposites.   The postulate of spiritual formation of the world appears as "thou shalt" in the consciousness of the individual Self which determines itself independently.

Art and science, too, as acts of formation, when seen in this way, have ethical significance.   That which deserves the name of a true state, must be more than mere politics.   Even might, "virtu", which Machiavelli considers the essence of the state, really means a creative acting.   The state, as a forming act of unity of the opposites of the many and the one, is, in itself, already a contradictory being.   Therefore, there is always a contradiction in the justification of the right of existence of the state.   But just this reveals its right of existence. Everything that really exists in the historical world, has necessarily in itself this contradiction.   Culture and civilisation arise from self-formation of this reality.   It is the understanding of the rose on the cross of the present; otherwise it would not be culture.

Art, too, is originally a self-forming act of society, as unity of opposites.   In this respect, the opinion gathers weight that art was born out of ceremonial conventions of society.   (Jane Harrison, "Ancient Art and Ritual").

232

And as far as art may progress, this [historical-social] character does not disappear. This is the reason why I call art "concrete-logical". The deeper the formation — in the way of unity of opposites —, the more various civilisations differentiate and develop in different directions; but all have as center the reality of action-intuition.

The world of unity of opposites, as I have said, contains in the process of self-formation from the formed towards the forming, something like idea and intuition, [something spiritual], but this does not mean unity and identity of the world within itself. If that were true, the world would not be one of absolute unity of opposites. In a world of unity of opposites, self-identity essentially transcends this world [of human culture]. It must be absolutely transcendent. There is [here] no path leading from man to God.

The individual many and the whole one never become one in this world. As long as one considers the spiritual as [mere] immanent self-identity in this world, one does not yet face the real world which truly moves by itself. Therefore, the world of unity of opposites negates even the spiritual and culture. A [mere] spiritual world is a world of illusion. Everything spiritual is subject to change and evolution; it has birth and death.

Since the world has the character of unity of opposites, the process of self-formation is essentially neither mechanical nor teleological, but of the kind of spiritual formation. Since the world is absolutely dialectical, it contains the spiritual and intuitive element. Therefore, it can be said that civilisation and religion join where

233

they oppose each other. This is the reason why I said, in my essay "The Standpoint of the Individual in the Historical World": "The world is spiritual where it mirrors a unity of opposites". As I have often said with regard to the act of expression, the fact that the Self mirrors in itself an image, is continuity of discontinuity, or continuity of the absolute break. It means that the total transcendent is immanent, contradicting itself, because it has the character of unity of opposites. Civilisation is not the purpose of religion. Quite the contrary! But, at the same time, all civilisation is born out of religion.

The world of unity of opposites has its unity and self-identity, but not in itself. Identity, as unity of opposites, is always transcendent for this world. That is why self-formation of the world, as determination without a determining one, is spiritual. The fact that the world has unity and identity in absolute transcendence, means that the individual many are confronted with the transcendent one, and that the individual is individual because it confronts transcendence. By confronting God, we have and are personality. The fact that we, as personal Self, are confronting and opposing God, means on the other hand, at the same time, that we are joined with God. God and we are in the relationship of absolute unity of the opposites of the one and the many.

As individuals of the world of unity of opposites, we are in the depth of our origin in contradiction with ourselves. This contradiction does not diminish with the evolution of culture; on the contrary, there it becomes

234

more and more obvious. In the world of unity of opposites which has its unity in the transcendent, the process of action-intuition and poiesis from the formed towards the forming, is essentially a human progress. In this direction, too, we do not join the absolute, God.

With God we are connected in our origin, for we are created beings. As [creating beings, as] forming factors of the world of unity of opposites where past and future, contradiction themselves, coexist in the present, our life has from the beginning this determination and destination: we touch the absolute. Only we are not conscious of it. By looking back, deep into the roots of our own self-contradiction, we turn and reach the absolute. It is an unconditional surrender to God.

This is conversion. Here we find our true Self through self-denial. Luther speaks of "A Christian's Freedom", and says that the Christian is no one's servant, and everyone's servant. Therefore, we enter the sphere of religion not through deeds, assuming self-identity in this world, but by reflecting on the self-contradiction of our deeds as such, and on the self-contradiction of our Self as such. In this way, we hit the self-contradiction in the depth of our Self, as existential failure and salvation. But this is not realized by ourselves, but by the call of the absolute! Self-denial is not possible through our own Self. (The religious man speaks of grace).

This is the reason why religion is considered unworldly. But, as I have said above, religion must bring about the rise of true civilisation. By confronting the totally transcendent one, we become personality. And this fact that

235

the Self becomes a true Self, by being confronted with the transcendent one, means, at the same time, that I am meeting my neighbour in the way of "agápē". Herein lies the principle of morality, according to which the Self is personality by respecting the other as personality. With this destination the world of unity of opposites, from the formed towards the forming, forms itself essentially in a spiritual way.

Religion does not ignore the standpoint of ethics. The standpoint of true morality is even based on religion. But this does not mean that one could enter the sphere of religion through the medium of moral deeds, i.e. by doing good deeds by one's own power. Shinran's words in Tan-i-sho"[1] have a deep meaning: "Even the good one will be delivered" [— not to speak of the bad one].

In our day some people are of the opinion that the goal of religion is the salvation of the individual, and that religion can not well go along with national ethics. But this comes from a misunderstanding of the true nature of religion. In religion, the question is not of individual peace of mind. Such a wrong interpretation of the "absolute other power"[2] is only due to one's own convenience. He who truly surrenders himself completely to the absolute, has, indeed, morality as his goal. The state, as moral substance, does not contradict religion.

---

1) "Tan-i-sho", "Book of wondering", compiled by Shinran's disciple Yuin. Shinran (1172–1262) was the founder of the Shin-sect of Japanese Buddhism.

2) The "absolute other power" means the divine power of Amida (Amitabha), in contrast to man's own power.

The oriental religion of Nothingness teaches that it is the soul which is Buddha. This is neither spiritualism nor mysticism. Logically it is the unity of the opposites of the many and one. "All is one" does not mean that all are one without differentiation. It is, as unity of opposites, essentially that One by which all that is, is. Here is the principle of the origin of the historical world as the absolute present. We, as individuals of the world of unity of opposites, are always in touch with the absolute, although we may not even say that we are in touch with it. It is said: "He who sees and hears in the present instance only what is to him clear and distinct, does not cling to a certain place, but moves freely in all ten direction".[1] In the depth of self-contradiction absolutely to die and to enter the principle "all is one",—this, and nothing else, is the religion of "it is the soul which is Buddha".[2] It is also said: "You who are listening to my preaching, you are not the four elements, but you can use your four elements. When you are able to understand this, you will be free to go or to stay".[3] This does not mean the conscious Self, which is merely an illusionary accompanying one; there must be an absolutely denying conversion. Therefore, this is an absolute objectivism, in contrast to spiritualism or mysticism. This absolute objectivism is the basis for true science as well as for true morality.

---

1) Famous words of Rinzai, the founder of the Chinese Rinzai-school of Zen-buddhism. This school has great importance in Japan.
2) Nishida means spiritual death and rebirth, as taught by both Christian and Buddhist mystics.
3) Rinzai

"Soul" does not mean subjective consciousness. "The inward, too, cannot be grasped". And "nothing" is still a relative "non-being" which opposes "being".

The world which proceeds, as unity of opposites, from the formed towards the forming, itself, has its self-identity in transcendence. Therefore, in this world, the individual is the more confronted with the transcendent one, the more he is individual. And the fact that he is, in such a way confronted with the transcendent one, means that in the direction of immanence, he confronts the [other] individual with "agápē". While we, moving from the formed towards the forming, are born historically in this world, we are at the same time always confronted with that which is transcendent to this world: we [ourselves] have transcended this world. Here, individual and world oppose each other. That is the reason why I have said: that, which is "given" us in action-intuition, penetrates into our individual Self, and tries to deprive us of our soul. It denies not only our bodily being, but our soul. Our relationship with it is that of confrontation and opposition, because we are individuals of the world which has its self-identity in transcendence. In so far as that which is "given", and is pressing us, deprives us of our Self, we are not true individuals which have their Self in transcendence. We must, therefore, affirm and defend our Self against the world. Here is the basis for the "categorical imperative" [Kant's]. This behaviour is, essentially, our obligation as individuals of the world of unity of opposites. Otherwise it would be only "hybris", as mere moral self-estimation. The more personal we are,

238

as individuals in this sense, the more must we be spiritually forming, moving from the formed towards the forming. In other words, we, as creative factors of the creative world, must be tools of the transcendent one. Here, "moral" has no other significance than "religious".

Since the world as unity of opposites has its self-identity in the transcendent, and since we are individuals by being confronted with the transcendent one, so we move increasingly from reality to reality, the more individual we are; at the same time, we always reflect and think, transcending this reality.

The world, having its self-identity in something transcendent, has the character of expression, and we, as individuals of this world, have the character of acts of expression. The world being formation in the way of unity of opposites, we are reflecting when past and future become one. Reflection means joining of past and future in the present. The standpoint of thinking is a grasping of the endlessly moving world, in this direction, as one present where past and future are denied. From the standpoint of thinking, the world is grasped as one single present, and as expression. But from this very standpoint of thinking, the world is apprehended as having its self-identity in itself. There, the world which contradicts itself is apprehended as not contradicting itself. This is the contradiction of the standpoint of thinking.

There arises a standpoint of pure knowledge, where thinking and praxis oppose each other. It can be said: the more the world as unity of opposites is spiritually forming, the more we as individuals are thinking. The

239

world, moving from infinite past into infinite future, and not having its self-identity in itself, is thought of as having its self-identity in itself, i.e. as "universal of conclusion". That is the origin of scientific knowledge.

The world, forming itself as unity of opposites, as has been said, is logically thought of always in the present of unity of opposites, as the universal of conclusion. The world has in itself the element of self-negation in this sense, and this is the reason why it has the character of unity of opposites. Otherwise it would not be the world of unity of opposites. But as such, it must be comprehended from the shown standpoint [of knowledge]; comprehending the world according to immanence and self-identity, means that the world is changed into something abstract.

Concrete logic contains abstract logic as mediation. But it is impossible to think concrete-logically from the standpoint of abstract logic. The world of unity of opposites cannot have its self-identity in itself. Self-identity must be contained as moment of spiritual formation of history, from the formed towards the forming, [in the moving world of reality]. Concrete logic is just where we as historical-productive Self progressively grasp reality. It can be said that here the world, containing us in the unity of the opposites of the many and the one, makes itself clear. Our consciousness, contradicting itself, becomes the consciousness of the world. Therefore, it can also be said that we are mirroring the world through praxis, and that things prove themselves. Although knowledge begins with abstract analysis, this, with regard to standpoint and method, is realized by self-reflection upon the standpoint of the Self, moving from the formed towards the forming. Knowledge is essentially a historical process. Self-consciousness of historical life is, in my opinion, dialectical logic. Therefore, science also, is dialectical. But it must be called "environment-like", because it sticks to the "from the formed". Therefore, it is quite abstract to look at historical life merely from the standpoint of science.

GLOSSARY

absolute   Nishida has a great liking for the word absolute. It should be read with emphasis, because it opens the mind to the metaphysical implication.

absolute, the   As in the philosophies of Spinoza, Hegel and Schelling. The absolute has the same metaphysical function as God in Christian philosophy.

abstract logic   Traditional formal logic, in contrast to dialectical "concrete logic".

acting   1) action in the natural world, 2) action of a self-conscious individual.

action-intuition   See "intuition".

basis   N. uses very often the word "bottom" similar to the German "Grund"; it is also translated as basis or depth.

Being   Signifies the absolute Being, or the absolute. See "Nothingness".

being   Signifies a particular being, or the general concept and essence of being and existing.

body   1) The biological body, 2) the "historical body" i. e. society or people. See "historical species".

bodily   Referring to body, mostly in the second meaning. See "historical-bodily".

bottom   See "basis".

character	Used by the translator in cases whenever there is no English equivalent to N.'s newly coined words: having will-character, the character of expression, etc.
concept	Logical term or notion. See "concrete concept".
conceptual	Conceptual knowledge, knowledge through consepts.
concrete concept : **concrete logic**	Concrete notion, in the sense of Hegel's "der konkrete Begriff", a subjective dynamic notion by which the objective concept or essence of things is represented. Also this essence itself.
confront	N. uses this word frequently. It means that two things or ideas are standing opposite to each other, having a dialectical relationship. The translator uses sometimes the word "oppose". Confronting something, equivalent to being confronted with something.
confrontation	See "confront".
conclusion	In the logical sense of syllogism. "Universal of conclusion", taken from Hegel ("das Schlußallgemeine"). This concept is of minor importance in these essays.
contradiction	N. has a preference for dialectical thinking. Contradiction, contradictory and negation are used frequently. The contradiction opens the mind to the presence of reality, and the special sphere of "being". "Absolute contradictory self-identity" is the literal translation

244

of "zettai mujunteki jikodōitsu", here translated as "The Unity of Opposites".

civilisation	Syn. with culture.
culture	Syn. with civilisation.
deny	Syn. with negate.
determine	Knowledge determines the object; being is determined by universal concepts.
direct	Without mediation.
depth	See "basis".
deepen	N. speaks of "deepening the meaning". When the meaning of a concept is deepened, the mind penetrates deeper into the essence, and gains a better understanding of the true character of things. N. therefore, makes a difference, between an individual and a "true individual", between acting and "truly acting".
envelop	N. uses this word very frequently. The Japanese word "tsutsumu", envelop, is also used for wrapping a paper-parcel. Sometimes syn. with enclose. See "lining".
essentially	N. uses this word very frequently, perhaps under the influence of phenomenology.
expression	The historical world has its effect on the individual not as a mechanical cause, and not as a biological purpose, but through "expression". This expression moves the individual to act, (similar to Toynbee's concept of "challenge"). The actions of an

individual are an expression of its will, responding to the expression of the world.

form, the
1) Form 2) equivalent to the German "Gestalt". Often used in the second meaning to signify form, appearance and structure of historical phenomena.

form, to
The verb "to form" is frequently used in the sense of giving form". The transition from nature to culture and history, implying human creative activity, is called: "from the formed to the forming".

formation
The process of forming.

general
Universal.

historical
Used in a very broad meaning, referring to the world of man, in contrast to the merely material and biological world.

historical-bodily
N. himself coined this word which he uses frequently. See "body" (in the second sense).

historical-social
Also newly coined and used with regard to the world of man, in contrast to the biological world in general.

historical species
Society or people.

intelligible
From Latin "intelligibilis", in contrast to Latin "sensibilis". "Mundus intelligibilis" is the spiritual world of Plato's ideas. According to N., truth, beauty, and the good have their "place" in the intelligible world. The intelligible world is determined by the "intelligible Universal".

intention

Psychological concept, signifying the basic character of acts of consciousness. The verb "to intend" and the adjective "intentional" are related to intention.

intentionality

Possibility or fact of intending by intentional acts.

intuition

1) Intellectual and artistic intuition as a high form of direct apprehension. 2) Sensuous intuition, in the sense of Kant's "sinnliche Anschauung": the "data" of the senses are given by (sensuous) intuition and formed by categories of the intellect.

"Action-intuition", a term coined by N., signifies the unity of acting and sensuous intuition; there is no action without intuition, and no intuition without action. Seeing and acting are one. Action-intuition signifies the spontaneous activity of man in cultural creations. Scientific experiments are good examples of action-intuition. As adjective: acting-intuitive, or acting-reflecting.

inward, the

The field of inner experience, but with emphasis on the metaphysical "Self".

inwardliness

Signifies the inward tendency of an introspective mind and heart. (The German "Innerlichkeit").

judgement

In the logical sense of a statement. "Universal of judgement" is a technical term of N., taken from Hegel's "das Urteilsallgemeine". It signifies the logical sphere of judgements, or the sphere of scientific judgements. Nature, as defined by science, has its "place" here, while psychological phenomena belong to the "Universal of self-consciousness.

line, to   See "lining".

lining   The Japanese kimono has a precious silk lining which shows at the ends. So the lining envelops, in a way, the kimono. N. uses this word "lining" to indicate the progress from the natural world to the psychological world and finally to the intelligible world. The higher sphere is like an enveloping lining of the lower sphere. The natural world is "lined" with the world of psychology, and this conscious world is again lined with the intelligible world. The innermost "lining" is the all-enveloping Nothingness.

mediation   N. uses this term in the sense of Hegel's philosophy.

nothingness   In accordance with Buddhist writings, this word is used for the common "nothing" or non-being. The capital "N" emphasizes the metaphysical implication in "Nothingness". Nothingness is the last "place" for every being, and, therefore, itself no "being". As the last and enveloping place, Nothingness has the metaphysical function of God in Christian philosophy.

248

outward	The outward world, the world of nature, as object of knowledge.
place	N. uses this technical term, taken from Plato's "topos", to signify the logical place of a term or a thing. Something is logically defined, when its "place" is shown. N's logic is a "logic of place", in contrast to the conventional logic of subsumption, where a thing or a term is defined "per genus proximum et differentiam specificam".
present	Present in time, in contrast to past and future; also: temporal present. N. speaks also of an "eternal present", signifying the eternal "now". The historical world is one single present, as unity of past and future.
reflection	N. uses this word in the positive sense of moral reflection, as well as in the negative sense of mere reflection according to the logic of reflection ("Reflexionslogik" Hegel), in contrast to dialectical logic.
resolve	Contradictions are resolved in the dialectical sense of Hegel's "aufgehoben".
Self	Syn. with ego. The translator writes Self with capital "S", to emphasize the metaphysical implication. N. shows in "The Intelligible World" how thought penetrates deeper and deeper into the Self, discovering the intelligible world of values, and finally the religious sphere of Nothingness.
self-consciousness	Consciousness in the strict sense of human

consciousness, implying self-consciousness.

self-determination Every particular being is determined by universal concepts. This determination is not arbitrary, but according to the logical structur of reality. There is no outward authority which would determine things, but all determination is self-determination of the universal.

self-formation There is no outward authority, forming the world; the world forms itself.

self-identity The principle of identity belongs to abstract logic. Self-identity signifies the unchangeable essence of things. The dialectical logic, grasping the ever changing and moving world, knows no static self-identity, but permanent flow. This moving and changing world has its self-identity in transcendence, i. e. in the infinite whole of the process, and not in a finite form.

shall The normative character of values is also called "shall-character", because the norm addresses the individual with "thou shallst!"

style of productivity Technical term, signifying the common character of natural, and especially historical creative productivity. This newly coined word is related to the "concrete concept" of things.

substance In the sense of Hegel; the state is the moral substance to which the individual will is subordinated.

250

substantial Adjective to substance. "Substantial freedom" is the freedom of the individual before
the law of the state, which is the moral
substance.

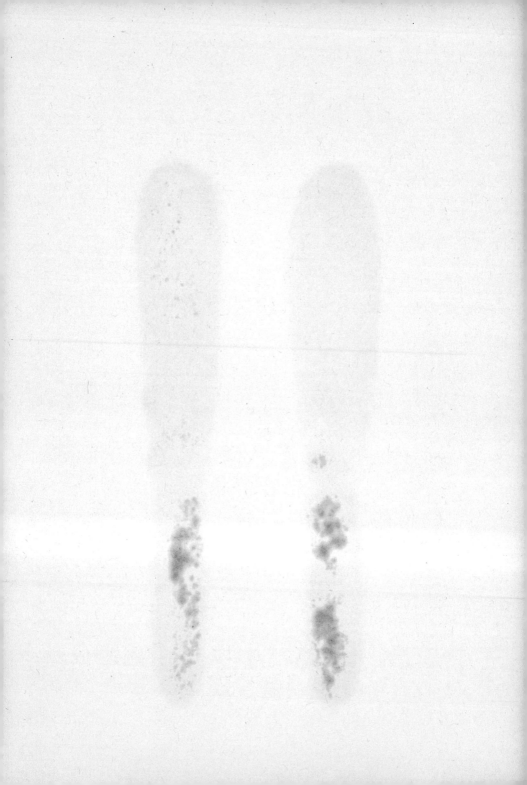

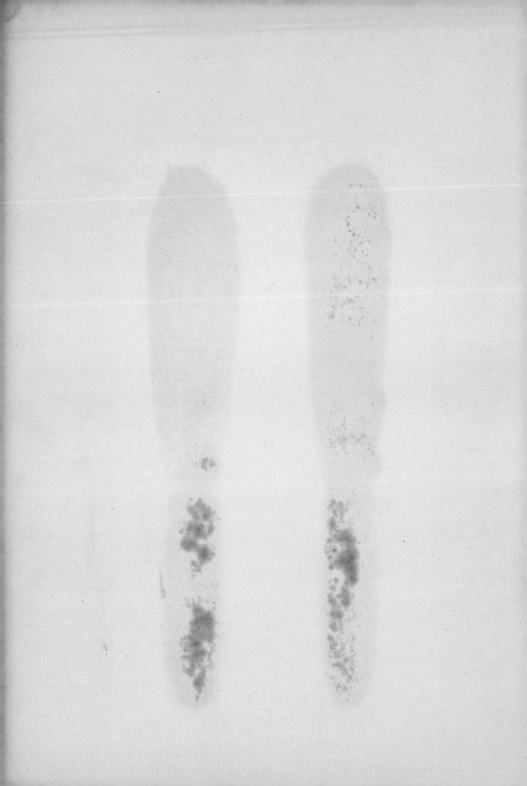

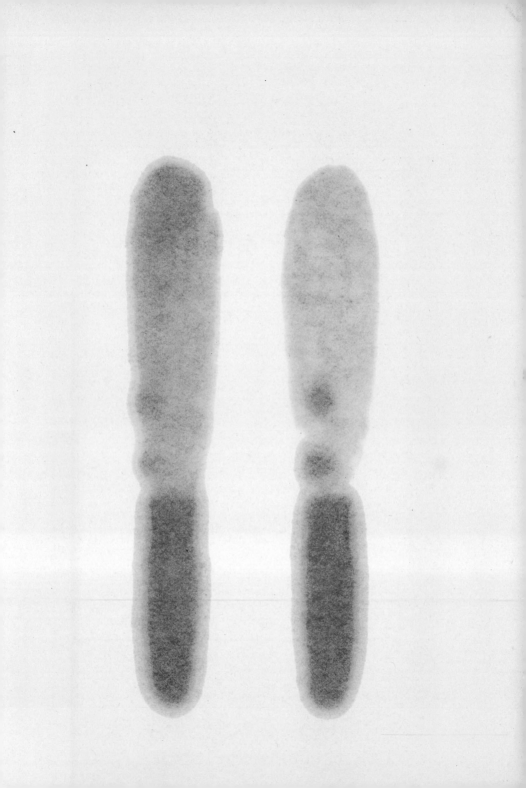

85320

B
5244
.N55
NA313
1966
O

Nishida, Kitaro.

Intelligibility
and the
philosophy of
nothingness.

HY

DATE DUE

GAYLORD   PRINTED IN U.S.A.